Composite Software Construction

Understanding SOA in the Context of a Programming Model

Jean-Jacques Dubray

C4Media, Publisher of InfoQ.com.

This book is part of the InfoQ Enterprise Software Development series of books.

For information or ordering of this or other InfoQ books, please contact books@c4media.com.

Managing Editor: Diana Plesa
Cover art: Dixie Press
Composition: Dixie Press

Library of Congress Cataloguing-in-Publication Data:

ISBN: 978-1-4357-0266-0

Printed in the United States of America

Acknowledgements

I would like to extend my permanent gratitude to Clayton Locke, Oka-san, Kojo-san, Satish Maripuri, Gopal Nagarajan, Martin Eigner, Ev Jordan, Frank Pritt, Jennifer Shettleroe, Michael Bechauf, Henning Blohm, Karl Gouverneur and Dave Green for giving me their trust and the freedom to make SOA a part of my life for the last 10 years.

I also would like to dedicate this book to the few hundreds of people that passionately contributed to the SOA standards with integrity and ingenuity. Without their hearts and minds no progress would have been possible. This book is the fruit of all the passionate discussions I had with them and I feel privileged to have met so many of you (I can only name a few, please do not be offended if you do not see your name:

Tim Berners-Lee, David Connelly, Patrick Gannon, Jon Bozak, Monica Martin, Dale Moberg, John Yunker, Jamie Clark, Sally St-Amand, Eric Newcomer, Martin Chapman, Stephen White, Bill Jones, Michael zur Muehlen, Roger Costello, Claus von Riegen, Colleen Evans, Jeanne Backer, Umit Yalcinap, Paul Brown, John Evdemon, Kevin Liu, Mike Edwards, Martin Reapple, Chris Ferris, David Frankel, David Orchard, Yuzo Fujishima, Gunter Stuhec, Robert Haugen, Tony Blazej, Paul Armond, Conrad Bock, Antoine Lonjon, Jean-Jacques Moreaux, Gregor Hohpe, Richard Veryad, Dave McComb, Philip Wainewright, David Webber, Fred Cummins, Nenad Ivezic, Francisco Curbera, David Chappell, Chris Kurt, Robert Glushko, Andy Roberts, Frank Leyman, Bill McCarthy, Todd Boyle, Dave Linthicum, Jeff Sutherland, Oliver Sims, Sanjiva Weerawarana, Satish Tate, Radovan Janecek, Philip Merick, Jeff Schneider, Kurt Kanaskie, Nigel King, Roman Stanek, Stefan Tilkov, Pim van der Eijk, Chris Bussler, Asuman Dojac, Fabio Casati, Vincenzo d'Andrea, Mike Papazoglou, Ugo Corda, Mark Crawford, Layna Fisher, Marlon Dumas, Akhil Kumar, Mike Marin, Mark Baker, Doug Bunting, Mark Little, Mike Lehmann, Francis McCabe...

This section would not be complete without thanking Boris Lublinsky, Jacques Serra, Jeff Schneider and Stefan Tilkov for ongoing discussions and their help in reviewing the draft. Many of their comments and encouragements made this book far better than it would have been. NoMagic has provided me with temporary MagicDraw licenses for UML diagrams. I also would like to thank Floyd Marinescu and Stefan Tilkov for giving me the opportunity to be a contributor to InfoQ.com by publishing this book and many of my ramblings.

Contents

Table of Figures

Foreword

Service Oriented Architecture (SOA) is often viewed as an IT savior. Whatever problems exist today, whether it is prolonged development cycles, poor overall quality of code, inability to meet current and future business requirements, etc. all of them are promised to be solved by advances of SOA.

SOA itself has been around for at least a decade or so, and it has made enormous progress during this time, especially in the areas of technical aspects of services interactions, including service communications, security, orchestration, service level agreements (SLA) support and so on. The bulk of SOA publications are focusing on the topics of designing and building services and making them communicate with each other, while each and every software vendor is busy inventing and implementing its own version of a SOA platform. On the other hand little, if anything, is happening with designing enterprise solutions using SOA. For most of IT shops it is still business as usual – design and development is revolving around specific applications. Although many of them have proclaimed a successful transition to SOA, in reality, services usage is limited to either purely system integration or application distribution. As a result, services design and implementation is centered on applications, rather than enterprise concerns, thus severely limiting potential advantages of SOA, most importantly service reuse. At the end of the day such approach leads to creation of familiar applications silos, build with new technologies. This inability to show significant improvements and cost savings leads many organizations to start questioning the importance and advantages of SOA.

As it often happens, the issue here is not with SOA itself, but rather with its usage by different people and organizations. The expected benefits from SOA usage can only be achieved when it is used at the enterprise level for the construction of enterprise-wide composite solutions. The challenge though, as the scope of SOA implementation grows, is the use of an overwhelming number of new technologies and concepts, which requires new approaches to virtually all IT function, including enterprise architecture, requirements gathering, governance, programming models, etc.

In his small in size, but huge in the amount of information book, Jean-Jacques takes us on a fascinating journey from today's software development and delivery practices to the state of the art SOA implementations. Welcome to the journey.

Boris Lublinsky

Chicago, August 2007

1

Introduction

"Connectivity" has been at the foundation of human innovation and progress for the last five thousand years. Transportation and Communication infrastructures have enabled a specialization and composition of human activities empowering each economic agent to use and contribute the best of its abilities. In the last hundred years, this movement has accelerated with new transportation means and today vertical industrial conglomerates have all but disappeared under the economic pressure of an agile, layered and dynamic fabric of enterprises of all sizes offering composable services to each other. Indeed, this fabric is itself creating tremendous competitive strains on its constituents by globally propagating innovations and optimizations. These permanent threats have created a need to continuously re-engineer enterprise processes such as design, sourcing, production, delivery, marketing and support. Furthermore, technological advances have shown their ability to wipe out century old industries within a few years. In this now global fabric, an enterprise must secure a decisive capacity to innovate, adapt and optimize or else, one of its competitors will quickly gain the ability to sell an equivalent product in its markets to its customers.

Paradoxically, the advent of the richest and fastest communication network combined with the use of the most powerful computers and high levels of automation have revealed a crying lack of adaptability of IT organizations, hindering new business models and relationships, while slowing enterprise productivity gains. As a result, IT, one of the major vectors of change for the past thirty years, can no longer be perceived as much as a competitive differentiator since the costs and risks of delivering new solutions make it difficult to follow the business cycles of an organization.

In the last five years, the Software Industry has started a major evolution of the concepts and technologies used to build information systems to both adapt to the "Connected World" and restore IT's leadership in driving business value. The foundation of this evolution is "Service Oriented Architecture" and its flagship is "composition", i.e. the ability to build assets that can be reused in contexts unknown at the time they were designed. Asset reuse and composition are expected to improve the response time and the cost of developing or adapting solutions while restoring the enterprise's ability to innovate, adapt and optimize. Technologies seek to achieve composition at the hardware level, with the concept of grid computing[1], and at the software level in several dimensions as user interface, business process and information composition.

Service Oriented Architecture means a lot of things to a lot of people, yet most people would not leverage SOA as a new way of building information systems. In this book we take a different look at SOA, we are looking at defining a service oriented programming model –a composite programming model-, not just as an architectural style. We address the question of "how do we build an information system from a set of services regardless of where they operate and who controls them?" The reason why this question is so important is because in 2007 the value of a solution is not longer defined by its intrinsic capabilities, data model and business logic, but above all by its ability to leverage functionality and data wherever they are within and outside the enterprise's boundaries.

You will not find here a detailed discussion on how to use SOAP, WSDL, or BPEL, but rather how they fit together. I actually assume that you have a basic understanding of these specifications. There are many excellent books[2,3] available on the topic.

You will neither find the description of a service lifecycle or governance processes, nor detailed service design guidelines. I will be focusing instead on understanding how to assemble services into a composite information system and which design patterns are important to create reusable services.

Section 1 is about understanding where we are today. I take a quick look at the best practices in information system construction in 2007 and how they shaped IT over the last 15 years. This section starts introducing the rationale for composite solutions and provides a series of questions to help understand if they are right for you.

In section 2, we will start painting the "Composite Solution" vision and evaluate which assets can be reused and composed into new solutions and how.

Section 3 is about understanding how asset reuse impacts the software construction process. What is changing?

In section 4 we will take a look at Object Orientation, Integration Technologies, the concepts of Service Orientation and the Web Services technologies and how they apply to a Composite Programming Model.

Not surprisingly, there is still a gap between these concepts and technologies and what is needed to establish a fully functioning composite programming model. So Section 5 spends some time looking at wsper, a service oriented, process centric, model driven composite programming model. I will also discuss how Business Process Management relates to the programming model and we will take a concrete example to illustrate its concepts.

Section 6 focuses on Service Design for reuse. I will share some of the design considerations and patterns that help constructing reusable IT assets.

Finally, in section 7, we will take a look at how to get started with a Composite Solution Factory.

2

Software Construction best practices in 2007

The Software Construction Machine

For the last 40 years, software construction principles emerged directly from computer science labs with little consideration for the specific needs of information systems with a notable exception, the invention of Relational Database Management Systems.

Figure 1 features a simplified representation of the conceptual (requirements), logical (architecture and abstractions) and physical (technologies) views of modern information system construction.

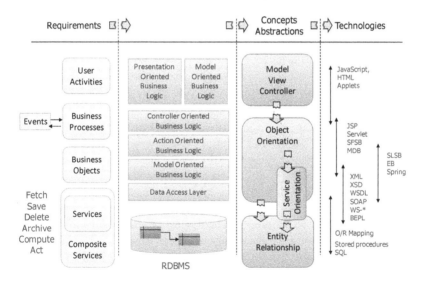

Figure 1. The Software Construction Machine

The software construction process starts with the definition of a set of requirements which are organized along the lines of functional and non functional requirements. However, and even today, requirements are captured with little formalism, they are usually a series of textual descriptions of what the system is supposed to accomplish and how it behaves, without consideration for existing systems and most importantly for future usage of the systems or the elements of the system.

Even when well defined business concepts such as user activities, decisions, business processes, events, business objects, services… are defined using formalisms (such as UML activity, class, use case, implementation, communication or state diagrams) these definitions can rarely be understood by key business stakeholders or even business analysts. This results in fuzzy specifications which often need to be amended during the software construction process as users start visualizing the behaviour of the system.

As the construction process continues, the architecture, the concepts and the technologies with which we construct systems are grossly misaligned with each other and with the way we can translate or use textual (or formal) descriptions into executable artefacts. All along the way, this situation creates opportunity for miscommunication and misunderstandings while making the overall process extremely inefficient and requiring numerous implementation patterns to avoid misusing technologies or combinations of technologies.

The architect is mostly concerned with creating a series of layers to facilitate both the implementa-tion and deployment processes while realizing non functional requirements such as security, scalability and fail-over. This state-of-the-art layering typically requires that the logic which represents atomic business concepts such as a business object or business process be scattered across several layers. Some attempts have been made to address this issue with the introduction of a "business component" concept[4,5] but they remain dependent on the current languages, programming models and technologies. One problem is that some business object validation rules need to be coded both at the presentation layer as part of particular screens (not even at the user activity level) and within the Data Access Layer. This is because the user needs instant feedback for mundane data entry errors and a server round trip is not practical. Some other validation rules need to be coded deeper in the architecture –hence in different technologies– because they can only be validated by comparing the data entry to other values held by the system, often depending on the action being invoked. Similarly, business process implementations are decomposed across the data, data access, action and controller layers in order to manage the business process instance's context, not to mention when a "business process level" controller is also in charge of implementing the screen flow to manage user activities as a unit of work with respect to the business process. This scattering process is devastating for the system's quality in terms of being able to meet the requirements, deadlines and expectation with regards to creating systems which can be changed easily. The pain is at its highest when your system needs to be changed on a short notice or a new release needs to be created to meet a large set of new requirements.

That's not all, if we now take a look at how a developer sees system construction, he or she is armed with a series of concepts, patterns and with a very large collection of disparate technologies that somehow need to fit within the layers of the architecture. Service Orientation has been thrown in the mix without much thought on its impact on the application architecture. As a mater of fact, for many, Service Orientation is a concept that can easily be reified in Object Orientation (Figure 1). The tragedy of modern software construction is that these few concepts with which a developer parses the requirements feature a heavy mismatch between them while the multitude of task specific languages have added to the misery. The ubiquitous Model-View-Controller pattern[6] (invented in the 70s) requires that "views" be constructed from the model to be represented in user interfaces, yet, object orientation is noticeably stubborn for not being able to easily create and transport views from a graph of objects to represent information in a way that can be consumed by the MVC view. SQL on the other hand is very efficient at creating some of the (flat) views that are needed by a particular user interface or operation. If your system is distributed and you absolutely wanted to use objects to transport your data, it would mean that each tier along the way would need a class library to "parse" the serialized data to be able to do something with it, creating maintenance, test and deployment nightmares and technology coupling to across tiers. The reality is that most developers do not use "objects" to directly carry data representations, even though they use object oriented distributed technologies such as CORBA, EJB, RMI and .NET Remoting with the familiar "Data Transfer Object" pattern.

The mismatches between these aspects and phases of software construction have driven most products or open source projects to focus organically on improving task level developer productivity while providing a platform that more or less can address standard non-functional requirements such as scalability, availability, security…

Yet, few software vendors are looking at simplifying the way we build information systems from requirement to deployment. I would argue that the profusion of technologies and the rate at which they are produced and evolved hinder even more the development of information systems.

MVC is a great technical pattern, but a poor information system construction pattern

The abstract foundation of all modern application models, the "Model-View-Controller" pattern -invented in 1978 at Xerox PARC by Trygve Reenskaug– is poorly aligned with the conceptual level of software construction:

MVC does not provide explicit user activity boundaries: the code is "unaware" of when a user activity starts, ends or reaches any other intermediary states. When a user activity spans more than one view, which is now almost mandatory, the developer needs to implement *ad hoc* state machines to manage the navigation between the different subviews, creating a coupling between several controllers. This particular problem has far reaching consequences, for instance if we consider a user activity based security model.

Similarly, a presentation layer developed with this pattern cannot interact natively with an explicit business process definition because MVC is following an "Event Condition Action" model that does not tie natively to the process definition. Implementations require dedicated code spanning multiple controllers that act together to perform business processes which makes them difficult to manage, monitor, change or compose within and across applications.

At the model level, the pattern does not provide a conceptual framework to create meaningful and reusable domain abstractions. Rather than representing a specific business entity, domain objects are often created to support specific views directly bound to the physical data model. As a result MVC model objects often couple the user interface and the physical data structure, not to mention when they blend in business process context elements.

The MVC pattern is an excellent technical pattern that can be applied successfully to implement GUI based frameworks and infrastructures but it is being misused to implement business semantics (business objects, processes and tasks). If you add the variety of technologies involved in its implementation (HTML, JavaScript, Servlets, EJBs, SQL...). It makes it difficult to re-use views, controllers and models outside the context for which they were designed.

Charles Simony – the only cosmonaut developer– compares the current software construction process to an encryption process where for example

400 pages of requirements turn into anywhere from 400,000 to 4 million lines of code, limiting traceability and coverage verification.

At the risk of being censored or bashed or both, I would like to express that this software construction machine is insane. Who would believe after looking at the machine this way that the assets produced can be changed easily when the requirements changes or evolve? Or could potentially be reused in other information systems? Now, don't get me wrong, this machine is good –maybe good enough– at producing infrastructure software assets, I am arguing here that this machine is absolutely terrible at producing information systems so critical to our economy. The misalignment between the business and IT is not just a communication problem; it is growing because IT cannot build the systems that the business needs for a reasonable cost, and here is why. This programming model leads to systems that are not:

- **Flexible** – when a requirement changes during implementation, vast amounts of code need to be changed and cannot be changed easily

- **Maintainable** – when new requirements are added over time, the programming model makes it hard to evolve existing systems

- **Reusable** – Capable of producing assets which can be reused in other systems.

Reuse is both necessary and hard to achieve. It is just as much a technical problem, as it is a discipline that requires governance processes to bring all potential parties to the design table. On the technical front, infrastructure software vendors focused on code composition rather than asset composition. Their libraries can be reused widely and often; yet, the assets produced with the utilization of these libraries cannot be reused across projects creating the need to duplicate assets. In turn it creates the need for integration to replicate data and state across these duplicate assets, while struggling to ensure consistent instance identity and security models.

If there was only one take away from this book, I would want it to be that "IT Assets must be constructed in such a way that they can be reused". This is easier said than done, and the goal of this book is to go beyond awareness and offer an architecture, a programming model, a set of guidelines and a delivery organization that promotes asset reuse. But before we do that, let's first look at how reuse impacts IT's ability to support the business.

The economics of IT

There is no better place to understand the inability to reuse assets than looking at the enterprise data model. Software construction has been productive enough and therefore cost effective enough to create a landscape where the data model of any given organization is "denormalized" and spreads across many systems. As an illustration, Figure 2 represents the attributes of business entities such as Customer, Order, Bill of Material... in different functional systems (ERP, CRM, SCM,....). This type of representation was first introduced by Dave McComb[7]. I am not arguing here for building solutions from a common database. Physical "denormalization" has benefits in terms of performance. I am really talking about the unnecessary spread and duplication of data attributes.

The major consequence of the lack of re-usability of IT asset is that it has been more cost effective to develop new systems and integrate them with one another, rather than carefully designing each system for potential re-use. This is a run-away system which can only stop when the costs of integration, operation and maintenance of all these systems overrun the IT budget. At this point the enterprise can no longer innovate, adapt and optimize.

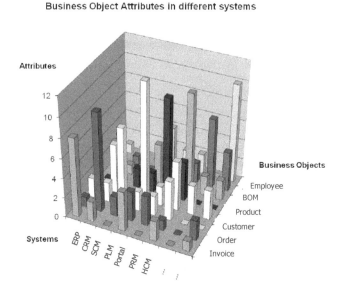

Figure 2. A Typical Data Model in Modern IT

In many organizations, Figure 2 is substantially larger due to geographically dispersed organizations, mergers and acquisitions... Furthermore, these systems are built over periods of time during which infrastructure technologies evolves, creating a de facto broad and complex technology landscape.

Figure 3 summarizes the plausible trends of cost and value of adding new systems to an IT organization versus the number of systems in a given IT organization (this figure is not based on real data but I believe we can all agree on the trends depicted here). At first the value increases rapidly because organizations automate high value business processes. Over time, the value doesn't increase as much because lower value processes are automated. It also becomes too costly to match all business needs (Figure 4). Business customers are often promised a v2.0, but it rarely happens because of the business value is usually lower and IT resources are always directed towards higher ROI. Overall, the complexity of adding these new systems remains constant but the cost increases because of the integration needed to replicate data and state to other systems of record.

It may also happen that adding yet another system could potentially decrease the value of existing systems: it is not uncommon to find information workers that utilize many applications to perform their day-to-day activities. This often lowers productivity because they need to switch context

Application-centric architecture creates islands of data and automation

Today's enterprise IT architecture is often viewed as a collection of applications. Design, development, enhancements, and maintenance of software systems revolve around applications. This approach leads to creation of segregated silos within the enterprise architecture, resulting in expensive and inflexible IT systems. Each application is built for a single purpose (such as loan origination, claim management, and so on), with its own data stores and for a single set of users. As a result, it implements only a subset of the enterprise functions, using and producing only a subset of the enterprise data, and typically without concerns about other processing within the enterprise. These silos manifest themselves as islands of data and islands of automation.

With **islands of data**, each has its own meaning or definition of enterprise objects. For example, while in one application "price" defines the net price, in another application the same term also includes sales taxes. Even if an object such as "address" has the same meaning in two applications, one of them can define it as a set of address lines while another one treats it as street address, city, state, ZIP, and country. Both cases create semantic dissonance between applications.

Each has information that overlaps with the contents of another island. For example, applications dealing with the management of health and dental claims also store the demographics information for the insured. At the same time, a customer relationship management (CRM) application contains both insured addresses and demographics. This duplication creates integrity issues.

None can provide a complete picture of the enterprise data. For example, a mortgage management application doesn't contain information about the borrower's loans from other lines of business. Creating a unified view of the enterprise data requires integrating information from multiple sources.

Each **island of automation** focuses on a limited set of activities within the enterprise (see Resources [6]). For example, the health claim management application deals only with the processing of health claims, without considering the role and place of these activities in the overall enterprise business process. This requires users to "application hop" to perform their work, thus impacting their productivity.

There is duplication between business processes contained within different islands. For example, an insurance company can have several claim-processing systems as a result of a merger or acquisition. This requires synchronization of changes between multiple applications, ensuring consistency of processes and business rules, supporting these processes.

The effects of islands of data and automation are invisible at the individual application level. However, they cause significant problems at the enterprise level, most notably with information fidelity and business process fragmentation.

B. Lublinsky, "Defining SOA as an architectural style" , DeveloperWorks, 2007, http://www.ibm.com/developerworks/architecture/library/ar-soastyle/

which increases the risk of inconsistencies between similar data inputs, increases training costs, lowers customer satisfaction... A company reaches this point when the cost of integration becomes prohibitive itself. This is when it relies on users to "finish" the integration between systems.

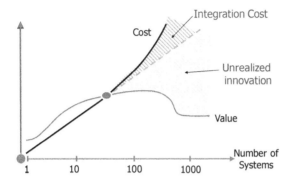

Figure 3. Organizations pass the negative ROI point as information systems are "denormalized"

The reason why IT yields less and less competitive advantage is because most organizations have reached the cross over point and have entered a situation where their financial margins can no longer be improved by IT projects. Even though many organizations still find innovative ways to improve their business or respond to competitive threats, the costs, risks and complexity of the existing IT landscape prevents most of the projects to go forward, or when they go forward the scope delivered in these projects becomes significantly less when compared to the business needs. (Figure 4).

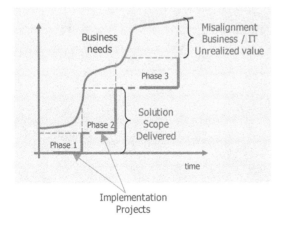

Figure 4. The gap between the business needs and delivered scope widens

There are three options from there. The first one is to consolidate or replace redundant systems to diminish the cost of change (Figure 5).

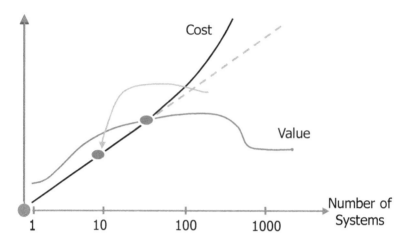

Figure 5. Changing the economics of IT: consolidate or replace redundant systems

The second option is to increase the value of existing assets at constant cost. The simplest and most natural way to increase the value of existing assets is to reuse them in new solutions.

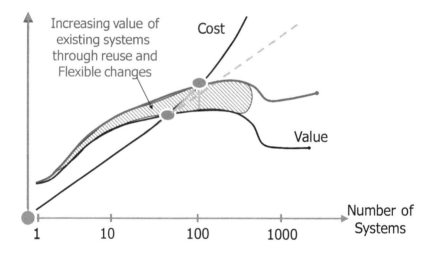

Figure 6. Changing the economics of IT: increase value of existing assets

The third option is to reduce cost which is achieved by outsourcing entire systems and operations, as well as custom development activities.

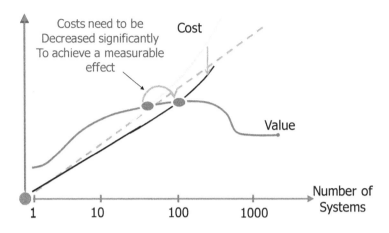

Figure 7. Changing the economics of IT: reduce cost

There is no perfect strategy and most companies will create a blend of consolidation, replacement, reuse and cost reduction that fits their objectives. Consolidating and replacing IT assets with assets that cannot be reused (option 1) is probably the least sensible strategy because inevitably the same causes will lead to the same effect. It is not by pushing the development and operations activities outside your organization either that your response to the needs to innovate, adapt or optimize might all the sudden become adequate: larger projects have an increased risk of failure or somehow cut scope exponentially as they get closer to the delivery date. When push comes to shove first mover advantage will almost always be the one that differentiates winners from losers, and that cannot be achieved by outsourcing.

As we will see all along this book, Service Oriented Architecture and a Composite Programming Model will help with all aspects of the strategy: consolidation, replacement, reuse and cost reduction.

Transforming the economics of IT

The question today is not if we need to fix the "software construction machine" but how soon can we do it. Nicholas Carr struggled with the imperative style of his statement "IT doesn't matter" in his seminal article in the Harvard Business Review[8] which shocked the establishment. He almost apologized transforming the statement into a question "Does IT matter?" when he published his latest book. The reality is that we must create technologies and information system construction processes such that "IT shouldn't matter". In this day and age where humanity is about to face its greatest and direst challenges, software vendors should sell technologies and solutions which foster innovation, agility[9] and optimization not hinder them.

The only way to achieve this objective is by changing fundamentally the programming model towards composition and focused on the production of composable –therefore reusable– assets.

Figure 8 represents the ROI of two projects which are composed of a set of services, processes, decisions and human tasks. Each project individually can provide some return on investment. However, if we have the possibility to reuse assets such as services, decisions, process components and human tasks across two projects the combined ROI of the projects may become several times higher. The great news is that the ROI keeps increasing each time the assets are reused in new solutions.

Even better, when these assets are enhanced without breaking their contract with their consumers, all solutions that used them benefit from these enhancements without significant cost or delays.

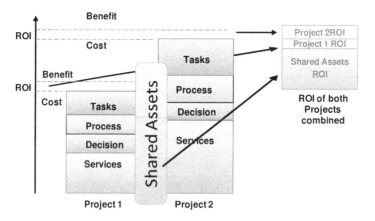

Figure 8. The economics of shared assets

Challenges created by inefficient software construction

I provide here a series of question that should help you decide whether your organization is ready for changing its programming model:

What is the percentage of your IT budget dedicated to?

- Innovate
- Respond to competitive threats

- Optimize existing business processes
- All the other activities

What is the percentage of projects requested by the business that cannot be accommodated each year?

What is the financial impact on your organization of not being able to deliver these projects?

What is the percentage of data that is considered to be incorrect (due to redundant entries, not enough validation...)? How is the bottom line impacted?

What is the percentage of your processes and activities which are out of compliance? What would be the financial impact on your organization if this was ever to become an issue?

What is the percentage of your processes that run on old, unsupported technologies?

What is the percentage of your systems that can no longer be changed without introducing significant risk since most of the developers have moved on to other projects or left the company?

What is the cost to your organization to maintain certain teams just to be able to change some systems?

What is the average number of systems you need to change in order to address the needs of typical solutions?

What is the cost to your organization of not being able to leverage 3rd party capabilities (business logic, data...) due to the difficulty of integrating with existing applications?

What is the smallest size project your organization can address in a cost effective way?

What is the cost to your organization of not being able to adopt technologies that exhibit lower production costs?

How efficient are the processes that identify potential optimization across your organization (discovery, measurement, prioritization, planning...)?

The reality is that no IT organization would be able to change significantly the answers to these questions without changing the architecture and programming model with which they construct information systems and solve business problems.

3

The Composite Information System Vision

Composite Solutions are assembled from existing assets

A composite programming model is a programming model where solutions can be built by assembling existing assets which may participate in any number of solutions.

A Composite Solution is ...
A solution which is built from reusable assets

Asset reuse can happen either at implementation time (library, object), deployment time (component) or at runtime (service).

A Service is ...
A runtime asset that can be reused, independently of the solutions which consume it

An asset can only be reused if its context of utilization can be defined independently of the asset itself. This sentence looks trivial, yet most information systems are designed as silos where systems of record and the processes that interact with them are tightly coupled preventing the reuse of these systems of record in new business processes. The coupling is so tight that the context of business process instances is often stored in the same tables as the content of business entity instances managed by the system of record. Ultimately, architects and developers implement a common data access layer between the business process context and the business entity content. As a result, these silos become hard to change on a short notice due to a change in requirements or maintain over time as the business needs evolve. Worse, the popular design pattern is to actually consider that the state of a business entity is part of the business process context.

A great candidate for a service is the Tax Calculation Service

A "CalculateSalesTax" service should be designed to be used in the context of an Order, Invoice, Quote, ... as well as across different legal boundaries (county, state, country) and any number of industries. From an IT operations perspective, it would be more efficient for the enterprise to "outsource" such service from existing business applications since the maintenance and management becomes shared across a large number of companies which otherwise would have to upgrade their systems each time sales tax regulations would change in their geographical and commercial areas of operations.

This of course works well because it is an "autonomous" business function, but the same remains true say of a "Purchase Order" service capable of being the system of record of purchase orders regardless of the procurement business processes that consume it.

The mere fact that an arbitrary number of assets can reuse another asset at runtime has profound consequences on the programming model. The traditional aspects of solution architecture may and most likely will become loosely coupled (Figure 9). This means that for instance the assets in which information is captured, computed, manipulated or provided may have been designed independently of each other and of the assets where information is recorded permanently.

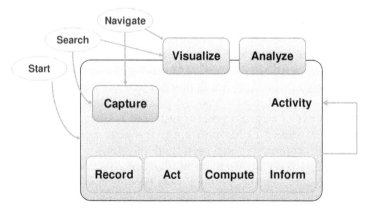

Figure 9. Aspects of the application model becomes loosely coupled

In addition, the services that compose the solution may:

- Live in independent technology stacks and be secured differently
- Scale differently
- Respond to arbitrary invocations from any other services, as part of different solutions
- Be replaced by another service without recompiling or even stopping the "system"
- Communicate via messages rather than using connections

Being loosely coupled also introduces a wide array of constraints:

- Interactions need to be contractually defined and evolved in such a way as not breaking the existing or any other solution sharing the same assets
- Changes to the "system" such as a data update cannot happen in isolation since all these services are autonomous. Some argue that these data updates may not even always be consistent[10]
- Concurrent invocations must be supported, while it is impractical to impose some form of serialization constraint.
- Security and privacy measures need to be designed accordingly
- Service should always be ready to start a new activity with one of their consumers
- Appropriate policies need to be in place to make sure a "solution" is "operational"
- Failure and Recovery become more complex

Another key differentiator of a composite programming model is the notion of "activity" which becomes pervasive. Service requests may come from different types of activity as the activity defines and manages the context of utilization of the service. Activities, i.e. interaction between services, must have a precise lifecycle. In the case of objects or components, the client controls their entire lifecycle, while, a service consumer controls the lifecycle of the activity, not the lifecycle of the service itself. For short lived interactions such as notifications or requests/response, the activity is implicit, for more complex interactions, the activity needs to be explicit with possibly a context of interaction associated to it. The context may either be shared, managed by the service provider or by the service consumer. Contrary to a popular belief, services are rarely "stateless": as they participate in activities, they need to actively manage their share of the context.

Information Services come in four types

- **Record**
  - o   Manage business entity lifecycle
- **Inform**
  - o   validate address
  - o   check credit report
  - o   check supplier inventory
- **Compute**
  - o   sales tax calculation service
- **Act**
  - o   Process purchase order
  - o   Reserve inventory, order parts from suppliers, schedule production, send advance shipping notice, provision shipping,...
  - o   Usually transactional behavior

Because interactions between elements of the programming model are explicit (and defined contractually) it becomes easier to detect and propagate events, especially as messages get exchanged. Today, most communication infrastructures implement an Interceptor Pattern[11] which enables the definition of events from the content of a message. The content of several messages may even be correlated to produce a "complex event".

A composite programming model has also interesting consequences in terms of "application boundaries": there are no visible technical or physical boundaries, only logical ones. A composite programming model typically exhibits a federated and collaborative point of usage where users can initiate, work on and complete any number of user activities irrespective of the information services or business processes they participate in. This point of usage can even be different for different users and support clients of any type (mobile, desktop...) more easily. In other words, different user activity containers may implement the same user tasks.

A composite solution is easier to evolve because of its factoring. Changes internal to the services are typically invisible to consuming solutions provided the new version of the service performs its contract as it did before (semantically, technically and operationally). Because of XML and XML Schema[12], services may also be designed to enable forward compatibility. Similarly, changes in activity definitions should have fewer side effects since they and their context are clearly separated from the implementation of the services themselves.

A composite solution exhibits little or no need for integration because it is not based on its own system of record. Information services are typically normalized such that when an activity needs to "update customer information" the business logic involved in updating all systems of record that hold customer information is not replicated in the activity definition. We will come back on this design pattern in section 6.

Mediation

No matter how well crafted a service can be, it can only be reused when other services are capable of communicating and exchanging information with it.

Hence when two services have been designed independently the probability of them being able to communicate readily is close to zero. Even if they were designed originally to communicate and exchange information, over time, these services have independent lifecycles which will lead them to a point where forwards compatibility cannot be supported which means that they will not be able to directly exchange information because the contract they once shared has been broken by a newer version of one or both services.

Mediation needs to be built in the service container architecture or within an autonomous –composable– mediation infrastructure.

Wherever possible, services should leverage common communication transport and protocols, common information syntaxes and common semantics to minimize the impact of mediation. As a form of mediation, they often need to expose multiple endpoints to accommodate the variety of transports, protocols, syntaxes and semantics to support multiple consumers and or implement several versions concurrently.

New programming concepts: messages, orchestration and assemblies

Scalable implementations (in terms of numbers of consumers) can only be achieved using a message based communication mechanism, as opposed to connection based. But that's not the only benefit of a message based communication mechanism. It also supports sophisticated interactions between services. They can easily exchange events, notifications, request/response or any arbitrary number of message exchanges in a peer-to-peer fashion if the unit of work they perform requires it. For instance sending a letter may happen with a simple notification (one way message exchange) between the sender and the post office and the post office and the receiver, or request/response if a return receipt is required or even a more complex pattern which would enable the sender to query the post office about where the letter is when this letter is mailed as registered.

Current programming models do not accommodate these scenarios because their interactions are usually polarized (client → server). Even though the MVC pattern requires that the view be updated when the model changes, in practice, this almost never happens. Surely, almost anything can be implemented in almost any programming language, but the question is how simple this can be made. The complexity of achieving such a simple capability in a traditional application model is staggering.

Since "message" interchanges are not well supported by current programming models, they do not offer any facility to manage the context of message exchanges either. There is a growing need to make the "message" a primary concept of a programming language and enable the runtime facility of these programming languages to provide standard correlation mechanisms to associate a message with a particular unit of work and manage the context persistence automatically, just like traditional programming environment can manage memory allocation and garbage collection without developer assistance.

Erlang

Erlang is a programming language that was invented 15 years ago at Ericson's Computer Science Lab which decompose a solution into (OS) processes which communicate by asynchronous message passing.

http://www.erlang.org/white_paper.html

Orchestration languages have emerged to fill this gap. The first one, XLang[13], was published around 1999 by Microsoft. It was shortly followed by the development of BPML[14] by the BPMI consortium (which is now part of the OMG) and by WSFL[15] which was developed by IBM. Today there is a standard orchestration language, WS-BPEL[16] dedicated to the composition and orchestration of web services. More recently, a new technology neutral initiative, wsper[17] was announced and aims at providing an abstract SOA framework based on a programming language which includes orchestration concepts at its core.

The concept of "Assembly" is an important aspect of asset composition. Assets, which are autonomous software agents, need to participate –i.e. be assembled– in several different solutions which individually define a context of utilization. A service implementation should be able to know in which assembly it performs based on a correlation mechanism. The service container should be capable of exchanging messages with other services utilizing the assembly definitions as an end point resolution mechanism. This is an alternative to traditional routing patterns supported by Enterprise Service Buses. Of course, it does not preclude orchestration languages to be able to deal with the exchanges of end point references as part of a message exchange.

This new class of programming languages has its own formalism: Pi-Calculus

The ubiquity of TCP/IP and the Internet has enabled many systems to communicate with their environment with great ease. Such interactive systems are actually becoming the norm. Surprisingly, most of the work to model these categories of systems has started fairly recently when compared to the theory of sequential algorithmic processes (λ -calculus) which is the abstract foundation of all modern programming languages.

The λ-calculus theory is about modeling systems which have no or little interactions with their environment. On the contrary, the $\square$ -calculus theory developed by Robin Milner in the late 1980s is about modeling concurrent communicating systems. This theory also takes into account the notion of "mobility" which can either be physical or, as in the case of B2B, virtual (movement of links between systems). I think we can actually relate the mobility to the notion of "change": change of business partner, business document format, capabilities, etc – any modification of an existing relationship between two companies may be associated with mobility.

J.J. Dubray "Automata, State, Actions and Interactions", http://www.ebpml.org/pi-calculus.htm

Loosely coupled coordination agents

An arbitrary set of services composed into a solution may not be able to perform just by itself the actions necessary to achieve the goal set forth by their unit of work without some level of coordination. For instance, the traditional technical services found in an application container or as a library need now to be implemented as coordination agents, i.e. a service which role is to coordinate the interactions of other services. Some common coordination patterns include:

- Event management via publish/subscribe
- Transaction Management
- Trust
- Analytics
- …

State alignment between software agents

The notion of state and state alignment is crucial to composite units of work[18]. When a service (as a peer) notifies or requires state changes to another service, we need to make sure that at the end of the interaction, the states of each service are aligned.

There is a common misconception that says that "all you need is Reliable Messaging". Aside from the fact that the WS-RM specification came very late in the WS technology stack, let's explore why it is not enough.

The OASIS ebXML Business Process specification created the Business Transaction Protocol (Figure 10) to achieve state alignment and non repudiation.

Both, request and response are followed by two signals *ReceiptAckknowledgement* and *AcceptanceAcknowledgement*.

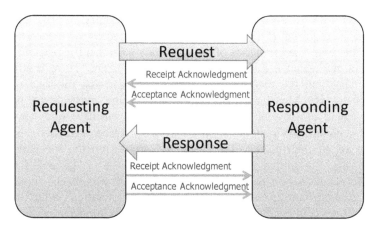

Figure 10. OASIS ebBP Business Transaction Protocol

A signal is a specialized message type. Signals have a format specified by the specification as such they should not entail any interpretation or processing error. This means that once the Reliable Messaging infrastructure tells you the signal got to the other side, it is unambiguously known that this side will be able to interpret the signal and will not possibly generate validation errors.

State Alignment in the real world

Let me illustrate the point with a personal experience. Recently my credit card company claimed that my account was delinquent even though I had signed up for a full monthly automatic payment. I called them to figure out what had happened, and the agent told me that they had sent me an email recently specifying that my 6 month period trial of online statements was over and I had to confirm I wanted to continue receiving online statement. It just happened that in the email they were notifying me that they would also interrupt the automatic payment if I did not confirm my online statement option (just as if the two were even remotely related).

This little anecdote shows that RM is not enough. The credit card company assumed that I got the message (otherwise the message would have bounced back) and that I had both read it and understood it, not to mention, they expected my memory span to be reach 6 months

A "Receipt" means that the receiver of the message not only got the message (as it would be indicated by Reliable Messaging), but this message was valid with respect to the expected schema. When non-repudiation is required (for B2B scenarios), the receipt is generally signed. In this case, the semantics of the signal are such that the receiving party cannot claim that it did not receive a valid message. Now, it still does not mean that the receiver was able to process that message or effectively did so. Many reasons could prevent the message to be processed: some of its content violates application business rules (not defined in schema), the system might be down ... Once processed, the application or an intermediary (in charge of processing the message) instructs the communication infrastructure to issue the *AcceptanceAcknowledgement* signal to the sender. This acceptance signal is called a non-substantive response, because it does not indicate what the response will be. It is just here to indicate that not only the message was received, that it was valid, but that the receiver was able to act on the message and effectively did so. Only then, can we claim that both sides are guaranteed to have their state aligned.

Logical View of the Composite Application Model

A composite programming model targets three aspects of software construction that have remained out of reach with traditional models:

- Leverage the business design information

- Support its evolution as efficiently as possible

- Be able to leverage existing assets rather than systematically building new ones

The goal of such model is to provide a solution architecture that is flexible, adaptable, and highly productive enabling a rapid and continuous alignment between the business and IT.

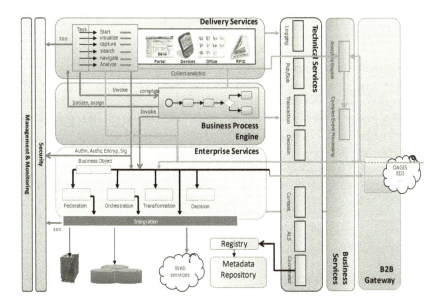

Figure 11. Logical View of the Composite Application Model

The layers of a composite application model are quite different from the layers of a traditional application model based on Java EE[19] or .Net[20]. A composite solution does not require having all layers in place to operate, though over time, as the level of maturity grows, most composite application runtime will be using a set of technical services, analytics services, security services and management and monitoring services.

The model is factored around three key concepts: task, process and service which each live in a different layer.

Delivery Services

User interactions are all performed within a task. A task represents a unit of work and can be standalone or participate in one or many business process definitions. "Search for customer record" is a type of stand-alone task which invokes services that help locate a customer record based on some information such as account number, telephone, address... A "Customer" service might have operations such as getCustomerByAccountNumber, getCustomerByPhoneNumber... which all can be invoked from the task based on the information provided by the customer. Once the task is complete, i.e. the customer record has been found, different business processes may be initiated: change address, cancel account, add features...

Tasks are managed by a task engine which is also responsible for rendering the user interaction in various technologies if appropriate.

Business Process Engine

The business process engine layer is at the heart of composite solutions. Business process definitions hold the solution's business logic which brings together a set of tasks and services to perform a specific goal. This is where the context of utilization of services is defined.

In a thesis published in 2007[21], Jungmin Ju retraces the history of business process definition standards. This history is long and complex, and not yet fully matured. Today, technologies are at a point where composite solutions can be built but it will still require several years of research to reach the full expressivity and flexibility needed to define and deploy enterprise class processes without the need to write code.

Enterprise Services

The enterprise services layer is where the core of work happens in a composite solution. These services are orchestrated by the business process layer or directly invoked from the delivery services layer (i.e. tasks). For instance a task "Update Customer Information" could very well be designed to simply invoke the "Update Customer Information" service. This operation invocation might generate events when specific elements of customer information get updated and need to trigger some business processes or simply other service invocations.

The enterprise services layer assumes that services are built from existing systems and applications, not necessarily from scratch. This is why the enterprise services layer is represented with a series of capabilities (data federation, orchestration, transformation, transaction, rules,...) and an integration layer acting as a container for adapters and connectors to legacy system.

The way the layer is represented does not convey the fact that services can be implemented in various technologies and in different service containers based on the capabilities needed. Service containers may actually be nested to compose their capabilities (if performance is satisfactory). From the perspective of a composite programming model, an "Enterprise Service Bus"[22] is simply a service container. The programming model itself does not mandate a proprietary communication mechanism as long as secured, transacted, reliable message exchanges can be achieved between the different elements of the architecture using Web Services protocols. However, it is likely that vendors will build composite application platforms on top of ESBs as they already implement most of the capabilities to deliver composite solutions.

Analytics Services

Because services, tasks and processes are loosely coupled they perform collaborative work by exchanging messages over standard transport mechanism and communication protocols. This environment represents an ideal substrate to collect analytics over the content of these messages. The advantages over traditional OLAP / Data Warehouse architecture is less integration required and near "real-time" detection of business events since it does not depend on ETL processes which typically happen later at night or even with a lower frequency.

Complex Event Processing

Some products offer "Complex Event Processing" capabilities using this new approach. CEP is particularly successful for fraud detection mechanisms which sometimes need to correlate several message exchanges and require instant response to block account transfers.

Technical Services

Technical services support the operations of task, process and service interactions. They offer logging, transaction, publish/subscribe… capabilities. They are often based on the coordinator pattern discussed in the Loosely Coupled Coordination Agent paragraph.

Security Services

Security services are paramount to the healthy operation of composite solutions and represent quite a complex problem to solve generically. A composite application relies on single sign on capabilities and principal identity propagation that enable services to operate on the behalf of the user with respect to the back end systems.

The business process layer help secure service invocation by controlling the context of a service invocation. However, it may also introduce some complexity as a service invocation performed by a process instance may not have a clear "user" associated to it. For instance, several people may have contributed to collect a customer information update. It is also not often desirable to specify the granularity of a service operation based on user interactions. This kind of coupling would result in less flexibility as this service is invoked by other types of business processes.

Management and Monitoring

While a composite application model is expected to solve a lot of the shortcomings of traditional application models, it also introduces some complexities. For instance, managing and monitoring the health of a set of composite solutions is quite complex. If a service becomes unavailable, what are the composite solutions which are impacted? Which business processes? Which tasks? How do we put work on hold until the service comes back? A composite application infrastructure requires a management capability that can stop and restart any elements of the solution without creating exceptions.

B2B Services

B2B services act as a gateway that implements additional capabilities seamlessly in terms of security, reliability, non repudiation... This gateway enables tasks, processes and services to communicate with the service interface exposed by business partners.

4

So what is changing?

Today's technologies, tools, methodologies and industry mindset are still based on a "build and integrate" approach. In this section we are going to take a look at how the concept of Composite Solutions introduces several paradigm shifts in software construction.

Achieve Business and IT alignment by design

Innovative companies have started to create a function focused on "business architecture". In fact, all businesses have a business design that describes how they operate whether this design is documented or not. The business architecture includes blueprints that describe how work is performed, information and goods are exchanged and ultimately value is created. It contains:

- An abstract information model
- The business processes
- The organizational structure of the people and assets
- The rules and policies that are associated with the decisions the business takes.
- The business' near-term and long-term goals and objectives
- The economic and market influences that affect how that business achieves its goals

Even informal business processes or exception handling contribute to describe how the business functions and responds to customer or supplier requests, opportunities, competition…

Many of those who have documented their business design have trouble keeping it up to date with what they actually practice. This is the challenge for funding such a project. Business processes evolve as businesses respond to shifts in the marketplace, regulations, or product innovations. This evolution usually happens without reflecting those changes in the formal design of the business and often without changing the systems that support it. This is a common problem in most companies. At that point employees often design the processes "around the systems" because there is simply no budget to keep the business model and systems synchronized. At this point, sticky notes flourish around computer monitors to capture the context of these "new" processes.

A Composite programming model needs to offer a number of capabilities that establish a holistic relationship between the business and IT:

- A formalism and language for capturing the business design
- A methodology for translating the business design into a set of runtime artifacts
- An infrastructure for hosting these artifacts that is as flexible as well as capable of leveraging information assets and business functions wherever they are hosted
- A place for retaining the correlation between the business design and the implementation that can be used to identify and fix failures to achieve the goals supported by the business design
- A means by which we can manage and monitor the system to ensure these goals are met.

Composite solutions must enable an organization to evolve the company business model at a lower cost, risk and project length.

The Composite programming model that we have described in the previous section is process centric, model driven and service oriented. It is process-centric, because processes are at the core of business models and the starting point of any innovation, adaptation or optimization. Service Oriented because, to lower cost, IT needs to reuse and leverage rather than constantly build new systems of record that require significant integration projects. Finally, this application model needs to be model driven to achieve new delivery productivity levels by enabling a direct translation of business requirements into implementation artifacts, with the goal of significantly lowering the development time and skills needed to build or change functionality. Tools don't improve productivity because they are "graphical", it is rather the adequation between the formalism they use to create executable artifacts and the requirement space in which solutions are specified which is the main driver behind development productivity gains.

To support a composite programming model, we need to develop a coherent set of tools and a repository where reusable assets that suit a particular purpose can be queried and found. We also need to select and deploy a composite application infrastructure which can now be procured from a few vendors or assembled from different vendors. We also need to establish a new set of software construction processes that spans project inception to solution operations (Figure 12) and drives new business designs from the business teams to the delivery and operations teams. These processes loop back to the business teams by providing operational metrics and accurate representations of the work being performed.

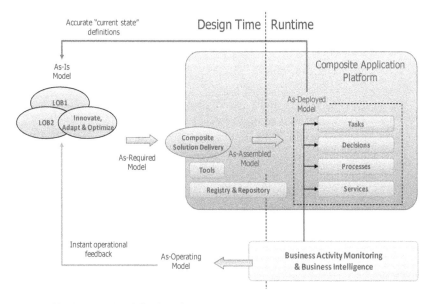

Figure 12. Business Model Lifecycle

The 4 capabilities the business would die for (that IT cannot provide today)

- Build solutions rapidly with small size projects
- Be able to visualize the business design in operation without complex "current-state" projects
- Be able to gain operational intelligence without complex measurement projects
- Be able to change the solution by changing the business design

I argue that the last capability is antagonist to the first three because it leads to simplistic programming models which are not well suited to meet the needs of the business. There is no need to transform your business users into developers except in very constrained cases when the parameterization of the business logic needs to change often.

The business can achieved far greater benefits if the first three capabilities where delivered consistently by IT.

Operate assets at the point of lowest cost

… not just solutions. The ability to reuse assets at runtime creates the opportunity to move these assets where their cost of operation is lowest. Composite solutions and services offer new levels of outsourcing, unlike traditional application models which require that an entire solution be outsourced.

In a composite programming model, services, processes (subprocesses), decision and tasks can be outsourced or sourced independently while the enterprise retains control over the entire solution's operation. Any combination is possible. A process can use tasks performed by outsourced personnel or invoked services that are operated outside the organization. I call this approach "right-sourcing" because it enables the enterprise to achieve the best ratio of strategic ownership over cost of operation.

Right-sourcing is about organizing and consuming assets, on-demand, wherever it is most cost effective to build, operate and maintain them. Assets which are common across an industry or even several industries are the best candidates for being right sourced. Figure 13 shows a taxonomy of assets which can be outsourced. The outsourcing of entire solutions cannot create as much unique value for the enterprise and lower the operational costs because the competition can acquire them as well. Furthermore, once a process is outsourced entirely, the enterprise typically looses the ability to strategically direct the 10 or 20% of the solution that could create a competitive differentiator. Today's outsourced solutions based on a Software as a Service (SaaS) model are likely to become over time a set of enterprise, industry and business services in a composite solution model. New competitive differentiators will come from the ability to retain the strategic assets and combine them with industry standard services. Right-sourcing is no longer focused on "core" and "non-core" processes like the traditional outsourcing model[23], it is rather focused on achieving the best possible competitive differentiators at the lowest cost.

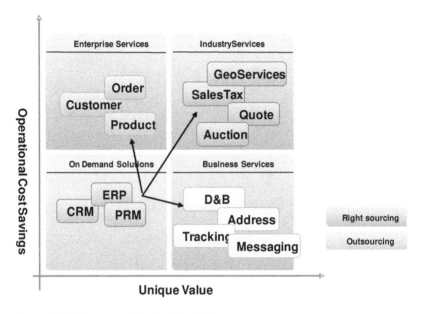

Figure 13. Software as a Service (SaaS) Taxonomy

A global sales tax calculation service operated by a third party could be used instead of updating this component within each system in every company each time a tax rate changes. Similarly, credit check, address validation… services which rely on large databases that are updated daily might be better off "right-sourced".

Deliver Continuous improvements

…not just projects. The key promises of a composite programming model are to:
- Enable smaller projects focused on ROI, i.e. "just in time implementation",
- Deliver business functionality faster
- Enable continuous improvement to meet business needs

A composite application model is expected to deliver solutions faster with smaller size projects because it is:

- Service oriented therefore assets can be reused,

- Model driven hence a large percentage of the requirements can be met with less code

- Process centric. Processes are one of the hardest concepts to code and test because they are complex finite state machines and they change frequently during the implementation as the scope of the "full process" (including exceptions) is discovered.

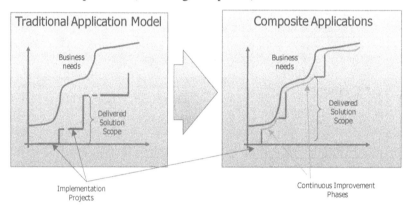

Figure 14. SOA delivers better business and IT alignment through continuous improvement

In addition, the programming model enable solutions to automate areas of highest ROI first as services, often with surgical precision. For instance, a project might start by developing a solution to simply monitor the operational metrics of a process (Figure 15). Once the automation areas that exhibit the highest ROI are identified, specific projects can be scoped to target these areas individually, leveraging the process implementation that was put in place initially.

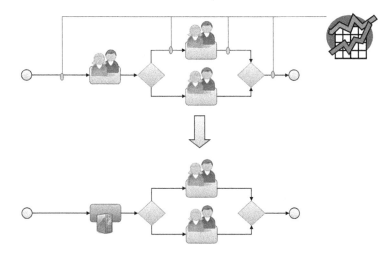

Figure 15. Monitor process first, automate areas with highest ROI

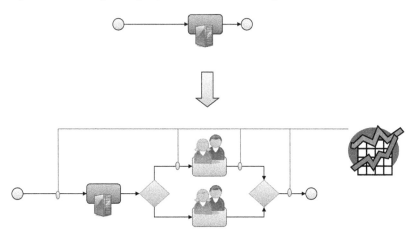

Figure 16. Automate first, then take control of the business process

Alternatively, projects might start by automating a task first and leave the rest of the process alone, and later augment the solution with full process management and monitoring (Figure 16).

Overall, a composite programming model, because it is process centric, enables continuous improvements with a lower cost and risk while targeting areas of highest ROI, achieving a higher degree of alignment between the business and IT.

Govern your assets

... don't just manage them individually. An organization cannot build reusable assets without planning and involving the current and future consumers in the specification and design of these assets. Whether it is about the security model, the performance, scalability, high availability or the interface design (semantics, schema and operations), all decisions need to be made not just for the present but projected into the future. Similarly, when an asset needs to be changed, the dependencies need to be analyzed and several versions of a service may be required to run concurrently to serve consumers which cannot be upgraded to a new version being deployed.

It is beyond the scope of this book to discuss the best service governance strategies in terms of organization and processes. This starts to be a mature field with many solutions provided by Infrastructure Software Vendors. These solutions are most often based on a repository and a service registry[24].

Many companies will start their service oriented architecture effort with different goals, budgets, expertise,... In any case, services need to be governed as early as possible in their lifecycle.. Design for reuse is likely to add cost to any given project because the service needs to be designed with not just the requirement of a given project, but also taking into account the needs of future projects. When creating reusable assets, my recommendation is to initiate individual projects or subprojects tasked to deliver just services while other projects deliver solutions consuming these services. These services projects should be planned ahead of the consumers to avoid being on the critical path.

Design towards the strategy and Goals

... not just requirements. The composite programming model enables a more direct association between solutions, the assets that compose these solutions, and the goals and strategy of the enterprise. In other words, the factoring of composite solutions and the metrics captured (or resulting from a simulation) can be directly related to the business goals.

In a composite programming model, the information flow and workflow are explicit, while the value flow can easily be computed via the analytics engine. Overall, traceability can be established from the enterprise goals and strategy to the project lifecycle from specification to design to operation and to the assets involved.

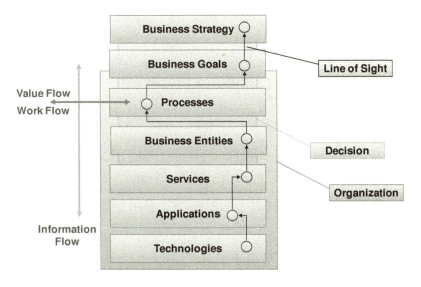

Figure 17. Line of Sight Methodology

Compose requirements

...not just assets. Solutions follow a large set of constraints which can be expressed at the industry level (or country level), at the enterprise level, at the business area level or process area level. It is only then that solution specific requirements can be expressed (Figure 18).

By definition, reusable assets should be designed without solution specific requirements while, solution specific requirements should focus on the assembly of these assets into business processes, and the construction of solution specific assets.

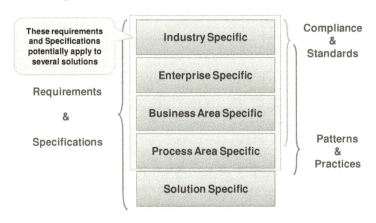

Figure 18. Composite Requirements

Select your assets

...don't just write specifications. A new, critical, activity is appearing in the construction processes: the selection of assets, which was often done at the infrastructure level in the past as enterprise architects would specify the list of preferred libraries, frameworks and technologies.

In a mature service oriented architecture, the solution architect will be focusing on selecting the appropriate services with the help of a query-able service registry and defining the corresponding service level agreements with the asset owners to support the new solution.

Think Contract and Quality of Service

...not just Functionality. Service consumers and providers are tied through a contract which often includes service level agreements that define the quality of service expected during the interactions. The contract can only be finalized when both consumers and providers are identified. Even simple services which expose a technical contract that can be considered unilateral need to set up specific authorizations and provision new resources for additional consumers.

As the number of consumers grows, it is expected that contract management will need to be automated to facilitate the onramp of new consumers.

Define Policies

...not just Rules. A policy is an assertion that describes one or more characteristics of the elements of a system. As elements of a composite application are assembled, policies can be matched and validated to make sure the assembly will perform according to the specifications. A policy framework supports a looser-coupling between the assets of a composite application because it allows for finding compatible matches that will enable the elements to work collaboratively.

Federate

...don't just expose systems integration points. Composite Solutions enable user interface, process and information federation. In a traditional –monolithic– application model, user interfaces tend to be duplicated across solutions because there is no possible way to reuse tasks or user interface components in another solution. Similarly, processes cannot be composed because they are not explicit and rely on ad hoc implementations that require specific integration to link processes living in different solutions. Information federation is also achieved via costly duplication of data structures and the use of replication/synchronization technologies (such as ETL).

It is only recently that Enterprise Information Integration (EII) technologies provided solutions to create a logical RDBMS on top of physical RDBMS. This technology is a great enabler of normalized service interfaces. The composite programming model is about bringing all necessary information and process touch points to the users to perform their tasks.

Assemble

...don't just implement. The concept of assemblies is the keystone of composite solution architecture as services are bound to units of work. Ideally, an assembly mechanism should allow the same service to participate in multiple assemblies. This can represent a challenge in terms of endpoint reference management and often requires the help of the service container. It was not until November 2005 that the first service assembly specification, SCA (Service Component Architecture) was published[25] as a draft which became a specification in 2007.

Certify

...don't just test. A service oriented architecture looks a little bit like a telecommunication network: you can never take it down entirely –nor do you want too–and you can never replicate it entirely either to perform tests prior to making changes to it. As you introduce new equipments or replace older ones, you need to go through a certification process (based on service level agreements for instance) to make sure that the equipment will not cause dramatic effect to the network.

A similar approach is required for building a service oriented architecture and avoid creating disruptions in composite solutions.

Publish

...don't just document. As new assets get introduced in a service oriented architecture, we need to publish information about them to a central registry24 such that potential consumers can look for them based on a taxonomy and a set of characteristics.

Provision

...don't just deploy. As new composite solutions are being built, the services they consume need to be provisioned based on their expected usage.

Think Threat

...not just Security. Monolithic application architectures are relatively easy to secure because they expose a well defined boundary materialized by a connection based API, few infrastructure elements and a simple topology compatible with a DMZ. Their database connections are dedicated and secured behind the DMZ. Once the code is protected against usual security flaws (SQL injection, Scripting and Buffer overrun) and as long as a user is identified with enough confidence, you are pretty much done.

In composite solution, there is a lot more to think about, and all the potential threats identified in the Microsoft's STRIDE model[26] need to be considered since services and elements of the composite application model exchange messages over standard protocols without the privacy of a dedicated connection and often well beyond the firewall:

- *Spoofing identity* — An unauthorized user impersonating a valid user of the application

- *Tampering with data* — An attacker illegally changing or destroying data

- *Repudiability* — The ability of a user to deny that he or she performed an action

- *Information disclosure* — Sensitive data released to users or to locations that should not have access to it

- *Denial of service* — Acts of sabotage that make applications unavailable to users

- *Elevation of privilege* — A user illegally gaining an unacceptably high level of access to the application

Data privacy introduces some important concerns too. Privacy policies need to be put in place to make sure that the consumer of some information does not break the guidelines for the data being exchanged[27] set forth by the service provider.

Summary

As we have seen, the changes introduced by composite applications in the software construction process are profound (Figure 19) and add some overhead to the construction process, undoubtedly. This overhead can be largely compensated by an improved communication and alignment between the business and IT as the solution design and implementation reflect and clearly link the evolution of solutions during a given cycle (as-is through as-deployed).

In the next section we are going to provide an introduction to the programming model via the concepts developed for Service Oriented Architecture and Web Services.

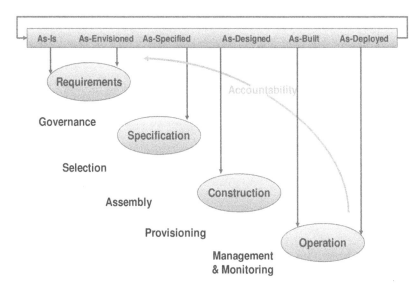

Figure 19. Composite Application Delivery Model

5

SOA and Web Services as a key enabler of the composite programming model

Object Orientation, Models and Runtimes

Object Orientation has been a way of life for many of us since the mid to late 80s and really became wide spread a decade later after the mid 90s. In 2007 it is all but impossible to write code that is not "object oriented".

The success of object orientation is due to its metamodel which is elegantly simple (Figure 20) and is well suited to decompose[28] and model the behavior of complex event driven physical systems. For instance, it has been extremely powerful to construct graphical user interfaces.

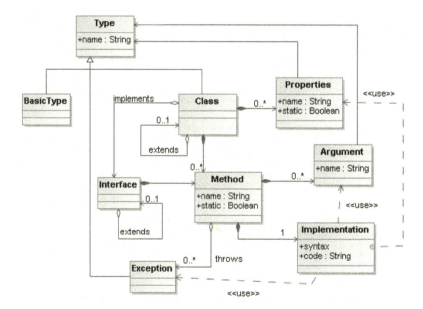

Figure 20 Object Orientation Metamodel

An object oriented run-time manages the lifecycle of instances based on the rules defined in the metamodel and provides some ancillary services such as code access security or garbage collection. A compiler would simply translate artifacts of the model (i.e. class definitions) into executable code linking it with the OO runtime libraries. Over time the needs of the developers have grown and runtimes have evolved to provide a large number of technical services. The architecture of web applications has introduced a separation between the runtime and the applications with the introduction of the application server and concepts such as "hot-deployments"[29].

Despite its formidable success, some concepts have remained challenging for object orientation. For instance, concurrency is not part of traditional object oriented runtimes, this is still an operating system level concept (which is often abstracted by object oriented API): threads need to be managed manually[30], and synchronization is the only way to deal with concurrent requests. If true concurrency is needed, an application server is required. Similarly, concepts like state or identify of an object are not generally part of the metamodel or the runtime. It is only relatively recently that Java and C# added the concept of events to an OO runtime[31]. Up until then events where handled by the runtime which would invoke the appropriate method on a specific instance. Historically, runtimes have also been extremely opaque offering no visibility on the operation of the application itself. It is only recently with the generalization of virtual machines and aspect Oriented Programming that some level of visibility has been possible by adding a data collector on selected method invocations for instance.

Objects have also failed to become flexible data containers as part of the programming model. For instance, you cannot query easily a graph of objects, nor create specific views (as another graph of objects) or transform a graph of objects into another with different class structures. Microsoft introduced the concept of the "DataSet" which is based on an Entity Relationship model. At about the same time the Java community created the Service Data Object specification (SDO) which serve a similar purpose but is based on the Hypergraph Data Model[32] instead of Entity-Relationship.

Sure object orientation is flexible enough, so much so that you can create all kinds of semantics within your application (such as a DataSet), in essence unconsciously expanding the metamodel and the runtime capabilities, but this is not necessarily a good thing since it does not enforce the separation between "business logic" and "runtime services". It also creates maintenance nightmare when these API change even by a tiny bit.

Figure 21 shows the basic ingredients of system construction: an application is a model which conforms to a metamodel with a certain number of code artifacts associated to it. The artifacts are written in a programming language the syntax of which combines elements of the metamodel and a series of standard control structures[33]. An application is deployed in a runtime. Both models and metamodels may be described using a modeling language (typically UML or proprietary alternatives).

In a composite programming model, a new reflective <<uses>> relationship appears at the application model element (as opposed a << synchronize>> relationship in a traditional application model) (Figure 21). As we have seen in the previous section, this seemingly simple change creates tectonic changes in the programming concepts, software architecture and construction processes.

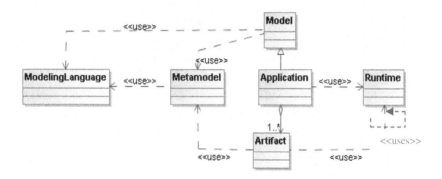

Figure 21 From Modeling Language to Runtime

Integration and Composite Solutions

Since Object Oriented Programming cannot help us directly, let's turn our attention to Integration technologies which have long been a critical function of all modern IT organizations which have often dedicated specialized teams to deliver this kind of projects. Since the mid-90s these technologies have slowly evolved from being batch oriented to support real-time[34] integration.

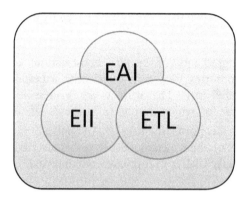

Figure 22. The 3 types of integration

There are three main types of system-to-system integration (Figure 22):

EAI, *Enterprise Application Integration* facilitates the integration of solutions via their integration API which is used to synchronize data and processes with other solutions.

EII, *Enterprise Information Integration* is used to federate disparate data sources (mainly relational). EII infrastructures enable the construction of logical (or virtual) databases capable of processing and dispatching queries to several physical databases, assembling results sets into a single result set and, if necessary, filtering this result set before returning it to the requestor.

ETL, *Extract Transform & Load* is used to synchronize large amounts of data between two or more data stores.

In general, both EII and ETL bypass all the business logic included the one in the Data Access Layer (DAL) that is otherwise invoked via the integration API of solutions.

Gregor Hohpe[35] has created a formal integration metamodel that summarizes all system-to-system interactions independent of the type of integration infrastructure (EAI, EII, ETL).

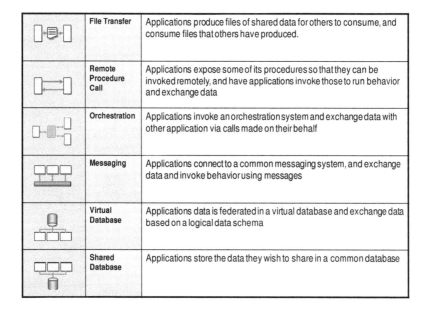

	File Transfer	Applications produce files of shared data for others to consume, and consume files that others have produced.
	Remote Procedure Call	Applications expose some of its procedures so that they can be invoked remotely, and have applications invoke those to run behavior and exchange data
	Orchestration	Applications invoke an orchestration system and exchange data with other application via calls made on their behalf
	Messaging	Applications connect to a common messaging system, and exchange data and invoke behavior using messages
	Virtual Database	Applications data is federated in a virtual database and exchange data based on a logical data schema
	Shared Database	Applications store the data they wish to share in a common database

Figure 23. Enterprise Integration Pattern (Source Gregor Hohpe, EnterpriseIntegrationPattern.com)

The only enterprise application integration patterns which intersects with SOA are "remote procedure call" and "orchestration". However all the EAI patterns, can and should be leveraged at the service implementation level when service implementations need to talk back-end systems.

If we look back at Figure 2 which features a prototypical data model in large IT organization, the creation of reusable assets is often going to happen along the lines of business object components (Figure 24). These services are classified as "enterprise services" in our taxonomy (Figure 13).

The general design guideline for enterprise services is that the interface should expose "normalized" interactions that isolate the service consumer from the details of updating every single system of record that manages corresponding business entity information.

EAI patterns can help implement these normalized interfaces. For instance a virtual database pattern could be used to implement an "update Customer Data" operation when multiple systems of record need to be updated and little or no business logic need to be invoked during the update. Similarly, a "purchase order" service would typically use the messaging or orchestration pattern to update purchase order systems.

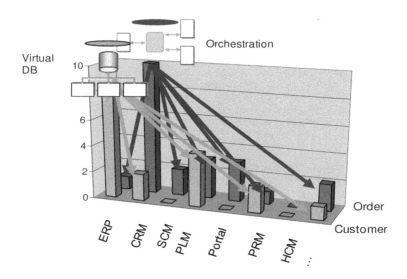

Figure 24. Leveraging integration patterns in service implementations

Gregor Hohpe also categorizes the message handling patterns in an integration infrastructure (Figure 25).

	Messaging Channel	How does one application exchange a message with another? Types of channels includes point-to-point and publish-subscribe. *WS technologies enable us to use an HTTP based channel*
	Message Endpoint	How does an application connect to a messaging channel to send and receive messages? *WS technologies provide end-point capabilities in all technologies (.Net, Java, Legacy,...)*
	Message	How can two applications connected by a message channel exchange a piece of information? *WS technologies use XML, a technology neutral syntax*
	Pipes and Filters	How can systems using different data formats communicate with each other using messaging? *WS infrastructure provide hooks to create processing pipelines and filters (e.g. WCF)*
	Message Translator	How can systems using different data formats communicate with each other using message *XML provides native transformation technologies, IBM WebSphere Process Server and Message Broker provide also native robust transformation technologies*

Figure 25. Message Handling Patterns (source Gregor Hohpe, EnterpriseIntegrationPattern.com)

These message handling patterns should also be leveraged at the service implementation level.

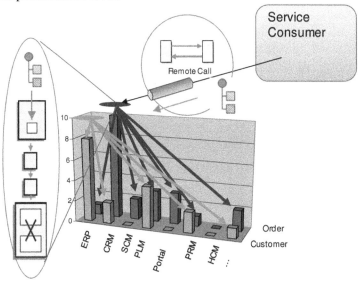

Figure 26. Message Handling Patterns and Service Implementations

Service orientation also leverages specific patterns such as the operation pattern (of which RPC is a particular case), the service discovery pattern, the dynamic routing pattern… which will be detailed in section 6.

Integration technologies like Object Orientation are perfectly good technologies to implement services but they offer little help if any as the foundation of a composite programming model. This is not surprising the <<synchronize>> relationship is conceptually very different from the <<uses>> one (Figure 21).

Service Orientation

A brief history of Service Orientation

Ever since Middleware[36] was invented, people have been developing reusable runtime assets. I would like to argue that Service Orientation really started the day someone got the idea of sending XML over HTTP[37] even though it is fair to argue that network accessible reusable runtime assets were built well before that time. I think, it is fair to say that the pioneers behind this kind of service orientation were BowStreet (bought by IBM) and webMethods (bought by Software A.G.). BowStreet was ten years ahead of its time. It had actually developed a complete composite programming model around the concepts of services, XML and XSLT by 1998, while webMethods was focusing on leveraging XML services for B2B integration and marketplaces. By 1999 the whole industry had caught up with some of these ideas and two stacks of standards, initially competing, were initiated: ebXML[38] and Web Services[39]. ebXML established very quickly a secure, reliable and transactional message exchange capability while optimizing the establishment of relationship between business partners via the concepts of:

- *Collaboration partner profile* which defined the capabilities of a partner (transport, security and collaborations supported)

- *Collaboration partner agreement* which defined the capabilities two partners will use from their respective profiles to collaborate

- *Collaboration definition* which defined the sequence of message exchanges for a collaboration between 2 or more business parties, as well as a non repudiable business transaction protocol to ensure the integrity of business transactions

- *Registry and repository* which hosted the CPP, CPA and Collaboration definitions

By contrast, the Web Services stack focused on SOAP, WSDL and UDDI only (without support for security, reliability and transactionality). SOAP was a transport independent message exchange protocol. SOAP was adopted by ebXML in 2001 which layered security, reliable messaging and transaction protocols on top of it. It is not until 2004 that security extensions were added to SOAP (WS-Security), and we had to wait until the summer of 2007 to get an interoperable Web Service Transaction capability, as well as a reliable message exchange specification... six years after ebXML published its first iteration of the specification.

The two stacks focused on solving very different problems: ebXML was definitely a B2B[40] standard focusing on lowering the cost of doing e-commerce and enabling smaller business partners to participate in electronic data interchange (EDI) which at the time required costly software and used of proprietary networks (Value Added Networks – VANs). The vision was to leverage XML and the Web to exchange information. The web services stack was focused on establishing interoperability capabilities between different technologies. At the time, this was a matter of life and death for Microsoft which had not been successful with its "DNA" initiative and was about to roll out .Net which has to work with other technologies to get a foot in the door of IT organizations. 2001 was also when the value of a given system started to be defined by its ability to integrate readily with its environment in addition to just its functionality. This is also when people started to realize the need for commoditized integration capabilities.

In addition, and in parallel the BPMI consortium, founded in 2000, focused on a new concept: an orchestration programming language. It was initially confused with the field of "Business Process Management" and still today, the dominant orchestration language, WS-BPEL which just released its v2.0, is still called a "Business Process Execution Language". In reality it is a programming language that can be used to implement services which interact with other services in a stateful way as we will see later. The confusion originates from the fact that a couple of constructs of the programming language look like some of the constructs used to model business processes. I hope section 5 will help you clarify the relationship between BPM and SOA and the position, albeit central, of WS-BPEL within a service oriented architecture.

In 2005, IBM and BEA introduced a new standard: Service Component Architecture (SCA) which, in combination with Service Data Object (SDO), greatly augmented the concepts of service orientation by adding an "assembly mechanism" to assemble services (service components, a.k.a as modules) into units of work. Web Services can participate in an assembly, alongside with a POJO[41].

This short history of Service Orientation demonstrates how chaotic the evolution of the stack of standards was over the last 10 years, squashed between B2B, BPM and interoperability. As of 2007, ebXML has become a mature technology but with little support from the big 4 infrastructure software vendors[42]. The Web Services stack is just complete with a good level of support for interoperability across all vendors. SCA just completed its v1.0 release, in record time, and is gaining some traction in the industry, except for Microsoft who seem to ignore how essential an assembly mechanism is to SOA and composite solution (but not so essential for achieving interoperability of course).

So even in 2007, and despite all the energy spent by dozens of standard working groups and hundreds of contributors, Service Orientation is still ill defined, and is still missing a service oriented programming model. Even the academic community, which started the first international conference on Service Oriented Computing[43] in 2003, has not funded a lot of research activity in this direction. Before detailing a proposal for such a programming model, let's parse the SOA standards and see how they relate to each other in the context of a composite programming model.

The SOA Standard Stack

SOA specifications from SOAP to SCA have been designed to enable software agents to communicate as peers in 3 types of scenarios (Figure 27). The first scenario supports peer software agents exchanging messages securely, reliably in a technology neutral way.

The second scenario is focused on formalizing the interactions between software agents. These interactions[44] are called services and require the definition of a service interface.

Finally, a large set of specifications is dedicated to the definition and performance of units of work (a.k.a activity) by 2 or more software agents. There is an important category of activities which is called "service composition" that helps expose new services from existing services.

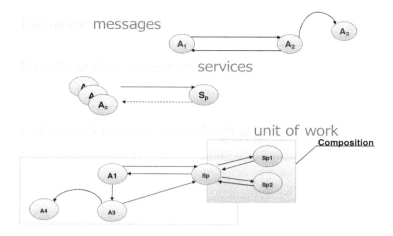

Figure 27. SOA standard enable agents-to-agents communication in 3 types of scenarios

The corresponding specifications that are required to support these scenarios are represented Figure 28 .

Other representations of the specification stack have been published here[45,46,47,48] but few representations are concerned with assembling these specifications into a coherent programming model. Actually, these specifications were developed individually by different groups of people, across several standard organizations, under the pressures of divergent political agenda. The fact that a programming model could emerge from such a scattered working process is almost pure luck since none of the major software vendors driving the specifications had made it goal. In fact, this stack is remarkably innovative. Having been part of many working groups I can assure you that every inch of innovation was hardly fought against scores of "old-guardists" who were pushing decades old ideas throughout the stack. The most ludicrous of all was the constant attempt to reify service orientation behind object orientation.

So before we detail at how the stack works and how it relates the composite application vision detailed in the section 2 (Figure 11), let's explore for a second how innovative this stack is.

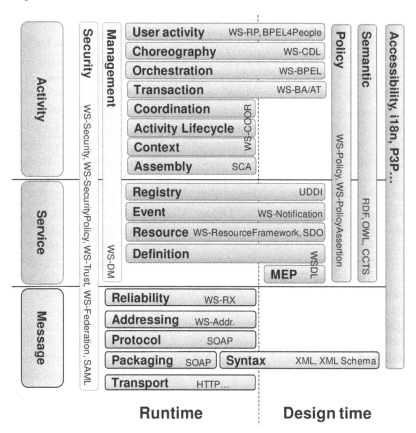

Figure 28. The SOA specification Stack

Extensible Data Structures

At the message level, the most innovative technology has been the XML standard stack which literally pulled message interchanges from the dark ages. XML is not just a technology neutral data format supported by a wide array of parsers. XML is the key to enable loosely coupled interactions between software agents. XML allows two agents to interact without requiring any agent to fully understand the structure of the message exchanged. This concept is entirely supported by XML Schema which allows for "open" (a.k.a. variable) content12,[49] and wildcards[50] when validating a document. Because well-formed XML documents contain both data structure (metadata) and data, they can be semantically accessible without the need for an interface: using XPath, a software agent can extract the elements it needs to perform its work. If the interaction requires a more rigid structure, there is still the possibility to easily transform an XML format into a consumable one using XSLT, either on the sender or receiver side, or leveraging the services of an intermediary.

But the wonders of XML's extensibility do not stop here. Well-formed XML documents are extensible, that is, data structure and data may be added without compromising the integrity of the initial document. This capability is critical in achieving both forwards and backwards compatibility when services are versioned[51]. This approach offers several benefits. One of the most innovative is the ability to evolve a business object instance. Unlike object-oriented or component-based implementations, XML instances can evolve from one schema to another or even hold structured data they were not specifically designed to hold, and can share any part of it. This makes them both flexible and adaptive. This notion of an "Extensible Object Model"[52] makes XML a key enabling technology in the construction of business process engine. The reason is because XML documents represent very naturally the business object representations (a.k.a views) that are part of the context of business process instances. With XML there is no need to create specialized database schemas to support specific business process definitions (as shown in Figure 29). XML business objects can embed traces of service interactions within the object itself without breaking the relationship between the document and the other services. In a traditional application model, the service would have to keep this information in a private store. In the event that another service wanted to access not only the information contained in the business object, but also this particular trace, the services would have to be integrated in the back-end to synchronize the object state. While this scenario remains manageable in a departmental infrastructure, it would be virtually impossible to synchronize the state in B2B scenarios where thousands of business partner systems that could potentially require access to this information.

This idea was first productized by eXcelon which commercialized a business process engine leveraging an XML database[53].

The extensibility of XML was only preserved after a long battle at the W3C. For some time SOX[54] (Schema for Object Oriented XML) was the leading candidate to define the concepts in XML Schema. Fortunately, this is now history and there is no turning back. The next version of XML Schema (v1.1) is pushing extensibility further based on the feedback of the v1.0 users. By the way, the use of XML to implement the context of business process instances is now a leading pattern.

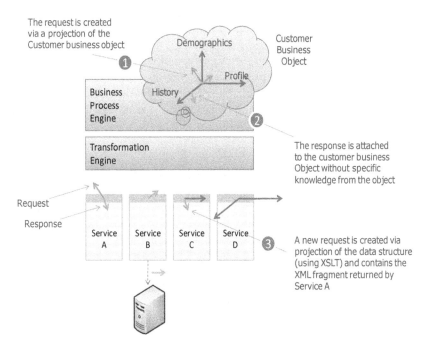

Figure 29. XML documents support the context of business process instances

I will not talk much about the transport layer in the context of the programming model because the trend in the industry is to become transport agnostic and select the appropriate transport at deployment time rather than implementation time. This trend was started by Microsoft with their popular service container WCF (Windows Communication Foundations). The Java community published a couple of years later the Service Component Architecture (SCA) which targets the same concepts. In the B2B world, the transport layer is critical because it has to be common to all partners to avoid costly intermediation. Again, from a Composite Programming Model perspective, B2B communications occur over specialized transport, via a B2B gateway. Should you need more information on B2B transports, Mark Yader and David Webber provide a great review in this presentation[55].

Injection of Dependencies

At the service layer, the innovation came from WSDL which enabled two software agents to interact without ever needing to exchange any kind of binary file. All that was needed was a machine readable service definition with the WSDL syntax. Of course, this is also possible because of XML and SOAP, but at the end of day, in 1999, that was innovative as compared to CORBA or DCOM. The second innovation has lost a bit of thunder since the generalization of the "Dependency Injection" pattern[56]. A service definition is designed to declare both inbound and outbound operations. Outbound operations point to dependent services which reference needs to be injected for every type of unit of work. This is again departing considerably from object orientation concepts which by no means provide a declaration of the references needed by an object. An object interface only exposes inbound operations. The Spring framework[57] was created to exploit this capability in the Object oriented world.

Sadly enough, WSDL was and is still designed with a flaw that prevents the usage of outbound operations and references. WSDL does not separate the bindings of an interaction from the interaction definition itself which prevents the support of multiple consumers when a description contains outbound operations. ebXML does this by separating the collaboration profiles from a collaboration agreement. This is a major problem because usually the interface description is specified well before one knows who is going to be a consumer of the service. Tragically, at the WS-Interoperability consortium, the decision was made to forbid outbound operations, rather than asking the W3C to fix this flaw. It was only the SCA specification that solved this issue, enabling peer services to be assembled in arbitrary units of work, not just client/server interactions.

Coordination

The third major innovation of the standard stack is the concept of "coordination" and two specializations of this concept named "orchestration"[58] and "choreography"[59,60]. Coordination technologies are critical because they enable a loose coupling between the software agents and they enable the composition[61] of software agents into complex activities which is essential for reuse.

A generic coordination framework was first and best described by the WS-CAF specification[62] (Web Service Composite Application Framework). It is unfortunate that this working group decided to stop its activities after the WS-TX specification was released because its architecture had far-reaching benefits well beyond web service transactions.

WS-CAF defined generically the concept of coordination as a set of loosely coupled services:

- A context management service
- An activity lifecycle management service
- A coordination service

As a set of services interact with each other, they often need a "context management" facility. Figure 30 represent an interaction between 4 services. It may happen that S3 requires the knowledge of the interaction between S1 and S4, while S1 and S2 were never designed (and generally cannot be modified) to carry this information.

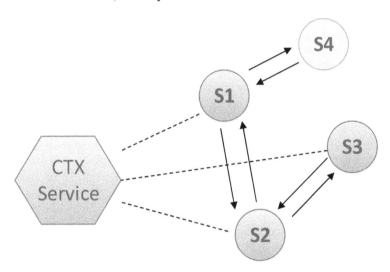

Figure 30. Context Management Service

WS-CAF's proposed implementation of the context service could be done physically via a specific context agent, or virtually by carrying the context at the SOAP header level.

Are web services stateless?

Web Services interactions as defined by WSDL are inherently stateless. There is neither a correlation mechanism to associate incoming request with existing sessions nor explicit session mechanisms to keep a context between interactions.

It does not mean that services MUST be stateless. Stateless interactions are always preferable when possible. Session management is particularly critical when you secure your service and a consumer makes repeated invocations to the service. The WS-SecureConversation was developed to avoid incurring the cost of authentication each time,

The second element of a generic coordination service is the activity lifecycle service (Figure 31). An ALS demarcates the units of work (at the instance level) performed by a set of services. Services are typically designed to perform an arbitrary number of activity instances simultaneously. Both a generic context and ALS service can help simplify their design such that each service implementation does not have to duplicate this functionality in a proprietary way.

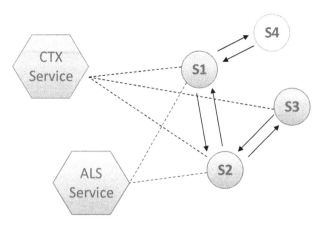

Figure 31. Activity Lifecycle Service

All kinds of coordinator agents (not just the one implementing a transaction protocol) can leverage these services to coordinate the activities between services. There are three types of coordination (Figure 32) based on the relationships between the services themselves and the coordinator.

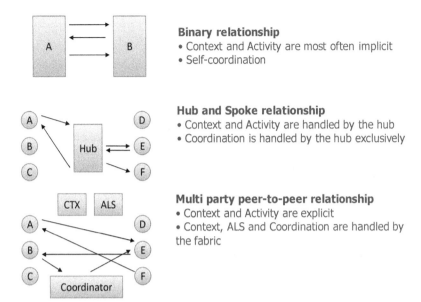

Figure 32. The three types of coordination

Orchestration is yet another innovative concept which is now implemented as part of the WS-BPEL specification[63]. The key advance brought by orchestration is the introduction of the "message" as a primary construct of the programming model.

Orchestration vs Choreography

An orchestration specifies the behavior of a participant in a choreography, while a choreography is concerned with describing the message interchanges between participants. Participants of a choreography are peers, there is no center of control.

A choreography definition can be used at design time by a participant to verify that its internal behavior will enable it to participate appropriately in the choreography. It can also be used to generate the service interface and an abstract orchestration that only contains the message exchange activities (receive, send, invoke) that support the interface. This abstract orchestration can be used to weave in internal activities to support the choreography.

At run-time, the choreography definition can be used to verify that everything is proceeding according to plan. It can also be used unilaterally to detect exceptions (a message was expected but not received, or help a participant in preventing it sending messages in the wrong order or at the wrong time).

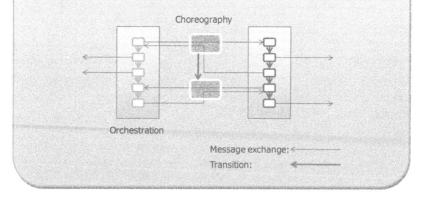

Up until know, computer science has been mostly focused on algorithms (data and control structures) while the construction of distributed systems relied on operating system level building blocks available through APIs in the programming model. There no specific constructs to deal with message exchanges. Because interprocess communication was the exception, this model was kind of working. Today, this simplistic model pushes the burden of dealing with issues such as state management (including state alignment), exception handling, concurrency or security for instance on the programmer.

State management alone can quickly become a nightmare if you consider that large organizations have hundreds of thousands, if not millions, of process instances routinely waiting for a message coming from the completion of an activity. These processes are of course running concurrently. Yet, no mainstream programming language ever tackled the problem of providing the semantics and a runtime to facilitate this kind of implementation for the developers.

Is WS-BPEL a programming language?

David Chappell provides a very interesting viewpoint:

D. Chappell, "Why BPEL is like bytecode?",
http://www.davidchappell.com/blog/2006/05/why-bpel-is-like-bytecode

> *People tend to think of BPEL as a programming language. The expectation is that a developer writes process logic in BPEL just as she writes object-oriented logic in a language such as Java. But unlike Java and every other mainstream programming language, BPEL is defined using XML. Accordingly, it was designed to be generated by tools, not written directly by developers. Whatever BPEL aficionados believe, masses of developers are never going to work directly in a complex XML-based language.*
>
> *In fact, as an executable language, BPEL's primary goal is to provide a portable description of logic. Isn't this exactly what Java bytecode strives to do? BPEL focuses on process logic, while bytecode takes on a broader problem space. Yet the two are quite analogous: both are tool-generated languages (bytecode by a Java compiler, BPEL by some graphical process design tool) and both can potentially foster portability.*

The way I would like to interpret Dave's comment is that he is not just talking about developers writing in XML using a BPEL syntax, he is rather expressing that even if you use tools, BPEL is not the right level to write your business logic. Yes, it is executable but you need better abstractions to write your business logic, this code will then be compiled in BPEL. My interpretation is supported by the semantic difference between BPMN (the business Process Modeling Notation) and WS-BPEL.

P. Giner "Bridging the Gap between BPMN and WS-BPEL. M2M Transformations in Practice",
http://wise.vub.ac.be/MDWE2007/downloads/giner.pdf

In all, Service Orientation creates a dramatic departure from traditional programming concepts, even though these technologies were "just" invented to facilitate B2B message interchange and commoditize integration across technology boundaries. Service Orientation relies on specific technologies which cannot be emulated easily by older distributed computing concepts, let alone existed decades ago. You often hear that SOA does not require web services, well this is as true as object orientation doesn't require object oriented programming languages and runtimes. Sure enough, most object oriented concepts can be emulated in C or Pascal, but at the cost of writing an Object Oriented runtime yourself.

Without reflecting deeply on these concepts and their impact, it is almost impossible to construct a service oriented architecture appropriately. I strongly refute the idea that people were building service oriented architectures 30 years ago, because they were not, none of the concepts detailed in this section existed in any way shape or form, let alone in a commercial product. And, if you needed on more proof that Object Orientation will be of no help to build composite software, please take a look at why OSGi[64] had to introduce the concept of "modules" (a.k.a bundles) which has the granularity of a Jar and very strict visibility rules as a key enabler of composite software.

Web Services technologies however require the definition of a robust reference architecture, a methodology and a framework to encapsulate the idiosyncrasies of the specifications and help leverage best practices. The sheer number of technologies involved demand a rigorous approach and training to reduce the immediate risk of failing service and composite solution implementation projects, but and most importantly, reduce the risk of not being able to evolve services as the number of deployed services and consumers grows to the point of being unmanageable.

The web services stack and the composite application vision

Figure 33 associates the composite application architecture to the specifications of the web services stack. Not surprisingly, the coverage at the technical level is good because the stack was designed to enable a set of software agents (services, processes, tasks, analytics engine…) to exchange messages securely, reliably and transactionally as well as assembling them into units of work.

However, at the programming model level, the gap is a lot wider. Business process definitions are not well represented by WS-BPEL.

BPEL is an orchestration language. It is unfortunate that its name contains "Business Process" because in itself it does not contain organizational information or the concept of "user tasks": the BPEL4PEOPLE[65] specifications had to be developed separately from WS-BPEL to introduce this concept as the working group was not unanimous about introducing these concepts in the core programming language.

Even at the technical level, the stack itself exhibits some shortcomings. WSDL 1..1 and even WSDL 2.0 do not offer a binding mechanism that supports outbound operations. So it is likely that WS-I will continue forbidding outbound operations for the foreseeable future. WSDL does not offer interface composition mechanisms either. It is possible to modularize a service interface by declaring that it extends 2 or more interface definitions using the WSDL 2.0 inheritance concept, which simplifies the management of large numbers service definitions (with WSDL 1.1 people had to use aggregation tools such as WPTA[66]). But the lack of a true interface composition mechanism means that WSDL definitions cannot be broken into the different roles that a service would play in an assembly and manage the relationship with each service independently. Two services associated in a unit of work will see each other entire interface. This creates issues for composite solutions at the service versioning and binding levels. When something changes in a service, you want to be able do an impact analysis that will tell quickly and precisely which related services are impacted. Interface composition would have simplified this problem as the minimal number of services would be impacted as a new version of an interface gets published. You may also want to be able to bind services independently of each other, i.e. establish binary agreements (with different SLAs) between any 2 pair of services.

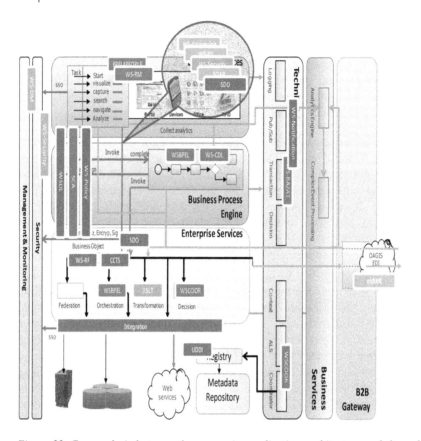

Figure 33. Gap analysis between the composite application architecture and the web services stack

Interface inheritance vs interface composition

[...] new to WSDL 2.0 is the concept of interface inheritance. According to [Anne Thomas] Manes, this "imposes an unreasonable constraint that doesn't correlate to real world services. There are valid reasons for multiple interfaces for services and it makes it easier for tooling." She said the working group was not unanimous on this issue.

"A majority of the Working Group saw the benefits afforded by this approach – the simplicity of the model, the simplifications it extends to bindings and the clarification of the role of WSDL," [Charles] Barreto said. "Even though there still are a number of WSDL users who feel that some means of stitching disparate interfaces together is a requirement, this approach confuses the use of WSDL in a manner that persists today. The role of WSDL is not to define service composition, but resources."

C. Frye "WSDL 2.0: Web Services' Lighting Rod Standard", http://searchwebservices.techtarget.com/originalContent/0,289142,sid2 6_gci1165063,00.html

Event definitions are not explicit in WSDL. WS-Notification[67] specifies the interfaces of notification consumers and providers but these interfaces have to be added manually to each service interface using the inheritance mechanism of WSDL 2.0 (which is not supported by 1.1)

The web services stack does not offer a business object concept at all. Service descriptions do not offer any way to specify that an operation message type contains a representation of a business object. Core specifications such as XML and XML Schema or newer specifications such as SDO do not allow for defining by themselves a full business object concept. They are rather technologies used to transport data. Even complemented with the WS-ResourceFramework specification[68], many concepts are still missing.

Not to mention the intricacies associated with the utilization of seemingly simple specifications such as WS-Notification[69]. When Microsoft launched WCF (Windows Communication Foundation) it touted that secure, reliable and transactional web service invocations could be achieved with a few lines of code and a small configuration snippet while a few years earlier, the same result would have required over 50,000 lines of code using the first generation of the Microsoft service container. However, WCF, which probably offers today the simplest Web Service programming model, does not address the "Activity" layer (Figure 28) except for the WS-TX specification and within the Services layer, WCF does not implement the concept of resources (WS-ResourceFramework) or SCA assemblies.

Even though the SOA standard stack, including the Web Services stack is close to delivering a programming model, the vendor interests are so divergent that it would be elusive to think that the stack will evolve naturally towards a programming model. So, if we want to further understand how to build composite solutions from this set of disparate, albeit innovative, concepts, I suggest that we go up a level and take a look at specifying a composite programming model. This approach is a lot more concrete than trying to go through all specifications and provide guidelines on how to use them individually or in combination with other specifications. Here, our intend it to define a programming model which artifacts can be compiled into SOA standard artifacts such as XML Schemas, WSDLs, or BPELs and deployed in today's service oriented infrastructures.

I have started an initiative to define this programming model as a formal specification called wsper ("whisper")[70].

Don't get me wrong…

I am not saying that the Web Services specification stack is useless or poorly designed. Sure here and there things could have been a little bit better. The stack itself does not have any product managers, it is rather a collection of vendors and sometimes individuals that decide to add a specification here and there to fill a particular gap, in a very specific context.

I am arguing here that the intent of the stack was never to create a programming model in any way, yet the technologies that emerged from the stack have sketched the foundation of a very innovative programming model, so why not go all the way? There is nothing sacred about Object Orientation and current programming models.

6

A Composite Programming Model

In this section we describe a new programming model, a composite programming model, dedicated to the construction of composite information systems. This programming model is called "wsper" which stands for Web, Service, Process, Event, Resource, which are some of the key ingredients of the language. Wsper is based on three main concepts: service, resource and assembly. A service manages the instance(s) of a resource type, while an assembly composes services into solutions.

Service Metamodel

Interfaces

Figure 34 introduces wsper's service metamodel. It is related to but differs from WSDL. For instance, a service may expose multiple interfaces while these interfaces can be redefined either by extension or restriction mechanisms. The set of service interfaces is called the "surface" of a service. Unlike a class, a service can only expose operations via an interface definition. An interface itself does not have private operations. Interfaces may either be declared public or private. We will see later that a private interface cannot expose any of its operation as part of a component within an assembly. Typically interfaces are defined along the boundaries of the roles that may interact with the service. However, this is not a constraint, but rather a guideline. An interface may interact with as many roles as necessary as part of an assembly.

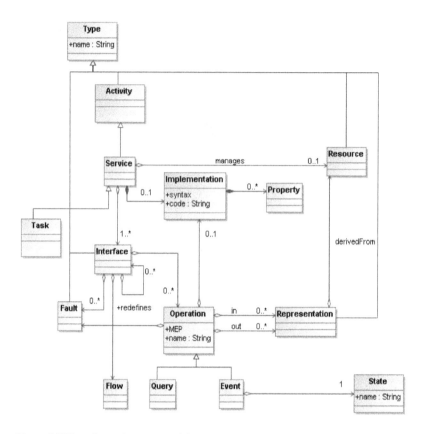

Figure 34 Wsper's service metamodel

Operations

As we have seen, one important distinction between an Object Oriented interface and a Service Oriented Interface is that outbound operations are explicit. In the OO metamodel, properties of type class provide a hint of the possible outbound operations that will be invoked, but they are not explicitly called out. Furthermore, object orientation couples the arguments and signature of a method when classes cooperate as part of a unit of work, which creates a thigh coupling between the two classes and leads to the utilization of the adapter pattern. In a Service Oriented Architecture, services are by definition designed in isolation, this is why, as we will see later, wsper's assembly mechanism implements a loosely coupled relationship between services using a concept of connectors (which implements data mapping for instance).

Wsper associates the parts of an operation invocation to a resource via the concept of resource representation. This mechanism is not restrictive in any way, it is simply designed to keep track of resource representations to provide advanced runtime services in terms of notification and replication if and when the corresponding resources change. Faults follow the WSDL semantics.

It is important to note that the service model does not provide any reference injection mechanism for outbound operations. References are defined and resolved either in the assembly definition or at runtime when appropriate.

Wsper specifies two additional types of operations: query and event notification (labeled event in the metamodel). Queries are difficult to map to service interfaces. One approach would be use to "Query-by-Example" (QBE) operations as necessary, another would be to specify a query language (hopefully not a new one) as part of the application model, associate a unique and standard query operation to the service interface which takes a query as an argument and make the service providers responsible for the implementation of this operation. Since in wsper the resources that are managed by a service are explicitly defined, the service consumer would have all the information necessary to formulate queries.

Wsper's event notification concept is designed to annotate some operations[71] such that they are able to leverage the runtime's eventing infrastructure. Some people have tried to create a separate concept "EDA" (Event Driven Architecture[72]) because the WSDL metamodel could not handle this type of scenarios. The reality is that it is totally unjustified to create a dedicated "architecture" just to be able to deal with events. The event notification endpoints references can be managed just as well by the runtime following a dependency injection pattern, injecting the event coordinator.

An event is the occurrence of a particular state. Since the notion of state is explicit in wsper, an event must be associated to a resource state. The event notification is automatically emitted by the runtime as the resource reaches this new state.

Implementation

Wsper supports both service implementations and operation implementations. This is again a major departure from Object Orientation which does not have any related concept. A service implementation, separate from operation implementation, is necessary because the units of work performed by a service are often stateful as we will see in the example later in this section, especially when a service manages the lifecycle of the instances of a business entity. In this case, the service needs to weave together a set of operation invocations that together advance the lifecycle of the resource instances. In this case, the operations are subsumed to represent the message exchanges between this service and the other services. Wsper provides a programming language that supports both service and operation implementations. The language is borrowing some of its control structures from orchestration languages such as WS-BPEL or BPML but more importantly tie together the notion of resource, state and service. In object oriented programming models, the concept of "service implementation" spanning multiple methods would have to be implemented manually by defining a correlation mechanism to direct a message to the correct object instance and by managing the state that spans several method invocations.

Tasks

Tasks refer to human tasks. From an architecture perspective they behave like a service which exposes a surface. However their behavior from a runtime perspective differs since there are specific operations associated to the task lifecycle or concepts such as "task handoff".

The surface of a task is not restricted to a single in-out operation. On the contrary, tasks should be able to invoke operations to perform queries, lookups... as well as exhibit a lifecycle that spans several operation invocations within the assembly.

Flow

A flow defines the behavior of a particular service interface. This is a concept similar to abstract BPEL.

Resource metamodel

A resource, in the wsper metamodel sense, is a type (it should be called ResourceType). Many instances may conform to a resource type. A resource instance is a persisted set of data uniquely identifiable. A service typically manages the collection of instances of a resource type. Some resource types may only have one instance.

Resource types maybe unstructured, semi-structured or structured. A structured resource type is called an entity. The structure is described following the SDO metamodel. In addition, an entity may have one or more state machines. The state machine describes the possible states of an entity instance lifecycle. Transitions describe the possible state changes allowed during the instance lifecycle. Actions may be associated to a transition and guarded via a condition. An instance can be in multiple states simultaneously.

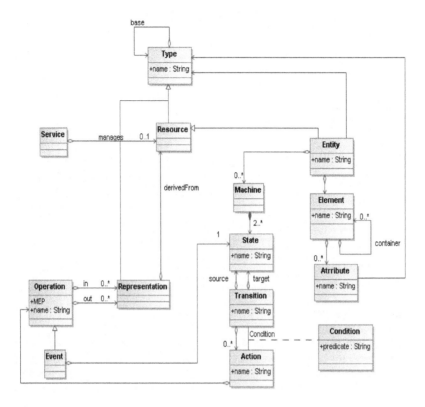

Figure 35. Resource Metamodel

Assembly Metamodel

Wsper's assembly mechanism is related to the one of the Service Component Architecture specification. An assembly is made of a series of components. Assemblies and components are units that can be deployed in a runtime environment. A component represents the deployment of a service in a runtime. In the wsper programming language a "service" is at the same level as a "class" in an Object Oriented programming language.

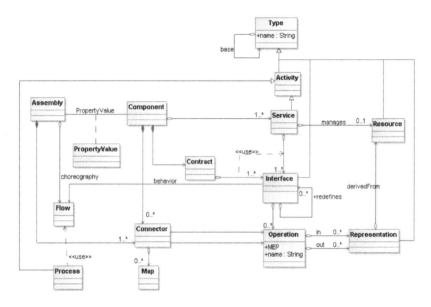

Figure 36. Assembly Metamodel

A component is composed of one or more services wired together via a set of connectors. A component exposes a contract which is a subset of the surface of its services. An assembly does not expose any surface while every component's surface must be connected for an assembly to be deployable. A connector relates two operations of complementary message exchange pattern (MEP). Optionally a mapping definition between the arguments can be specified to be deployed appropriately.

In wsper, an assembly may be associated to a flow that describes the sequence of messages exchanged by all components. This type of flow is commonly referred to as a choreography, which typically maps to a business process. A choreography itself is not a business process definition.

Packages

Model elements are defined in packages.

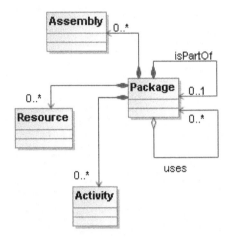

Packages utilize declaratively other packages, and of course packages are structured in a familiar nested structure. The "uses" concept is defined to avoid circular references. When a package uses another package it cannot be used itself by this package or any of its parents. A package may use any artifact declared in one of its parent.

Example

Scenario: a job application system

The job application system allows a candidate to create and submit an application. The reviewer would then review the application and request interviews if the candidate is selected. Interviewer should be able to provide their feedback. If the candidate is accepted, an offer should be sent and if the candidate accepts it, his information should be passed to the hiring system.

The main entity in this application is the Application entity which contains all the relevant job application information about the candidate.

Entity Definitions

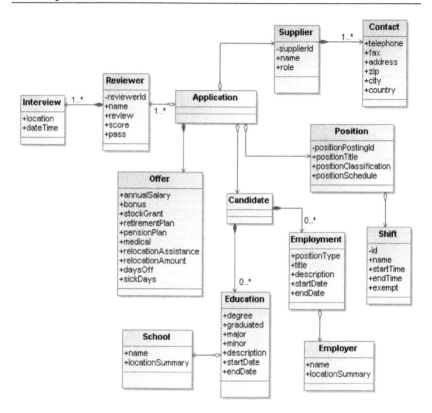

Figure 37. Application Entity Data Model

The corresponding state machine of the application entity is represented in Figure 38.

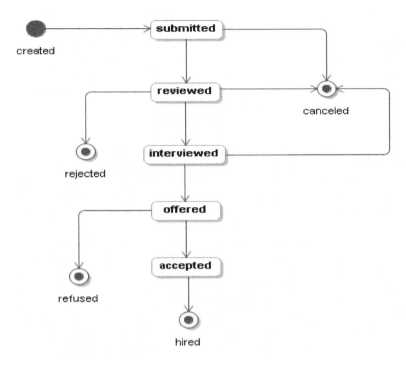

Figure 38. Application Entity State Machine

In this section we use a syntax that was designed as part of wsper's primer[73] and that is non normative, it is used to illustrate the concepts of the language.

```
entity application
{
  element application
  {
    string positionPostingId;
    string positionTitle;
    enum positionClassification { "Direct Hire", "Referal"};
    enum positionSchedule {"Full Time","Part Time", "Contract"};
    element shift
    {
      string id;
      enum name { "Morning","Afternoon","Day","Night"};
      time startTime;
      time endTime;
      bool exempt;
    }
    element supplier
    {
      string id;
      string name;
      enum role { "Recruiter", "Website"} ;
```

```
        element contact
        {
                element telephone, fax : org.un.ccts.phoneNumber;


        }
}


//The candidate element is open content
open element candidate
{
    string personName;
    string preferredPositionId;
    element employmentHistory[0..n]
    {
                element employerOrg
                        {
                        string employerOrgName;
                        element employerContactInfo
                        {
                            element locationSummary : location;
                            string organizationName;
                            }
                }
                string positionType;
                string title;
                string description;
                date startDate;
                date endDate;
    }
    element educationHistory[0..n]
    {
                enum schoolType {"University","Community College",
                        "TechnicalUniversity","HighSchool"}
                element school
                {
                        string name;
                        element locationSummary : location;
                }
                string degree;
                boolean graduated;
                string major;
                string minor;
                string description;
                date startDate;
                date endDate;
    }
}

element reviewer[1..n]
{
    string reviewerId;
    element interview[1..n]
    {
                string location;
                datetime dateAndTime;
    }
                string reviewerName;
                string review;
                int score;
```

```
            bool pass;
    }


element offer
{
        float annualSalary;
        float bonus;
        float stockGrant;
        bool retirementPlan;
        bool pensionPlan;
        bool medical;
        element relocationAssistance
        {
                bool provided;
                float amount;
        }
        int daysOff;
        int sickDays;
    }
}


machine lifecycle
{
    protected start state created;
    protected state submitted;
    protected state reviewed;
    protected fault state canceled;
    protected fault state rejected;
    local state interviewScheduled;
    protected state offered;
    protected state accepted;
    protected fault state refused;
    protected end state hired;

    transition(created,submitted);
    transition(created,canceled);
    transition(submitted,canceled);
    transition(submitted,reviewed);
    transition(reviewed,rejected);
    transition(reviewed,interviewScheduled);
    transition(interviewScheduled,rejected);
    transition(interviewScheduled,offered);
    transition(offered,refused);
    transition(offered,hired);
    }
}
```

Service Definitions

The service definition contains both the service surface definition as well as the implementation of the service and/or its operation. There is no need to declare abstract interfaces for 3rd party components and services since the surface of a service interacting with these other services should have the corresponding interface defined within its definition.

Surface

The job "application" service surface is composed of several interfaces:

a. The main interface which specifies the operations that control the job application lifecycle

b. A scheduler interface that is used to schedule interviews

c. A background check interface that is used during the review process to check the background of the candidate using an external service

d. The employee interface which supports the interactions with the recruiter and interviewers

e. The Data Access Service (DAS) interface, which is private, which means that none of its operation can be exposed at the component surface level. These operations need to be wired within a component between two services.

```
package org.wsper.demo.hr.application
{
  uses {
    package org.wsper.demo.util;
  }


  service application manages application
  {
    public interface application
    {
      Operation confirm create(application):invalidApplication(application)
      {
          MEP = In-Out;
          requires = {das.validate,das.update};
      }

      operation confirm update(application):invalidApplication(application)
      {
          MEP = In-Out;
          requires = {das.validate,das.update};
      }

      operation confirm process(application):invalidApplication(application)
      {
          MEP = In-Out;
          requires = {das.validate,das.update};
      }

      operation confirm offer(application):invalidApplication(application)
      {
          MEP = Out-In;

      }

      operation confirm acceptOffer(application):invalidApplication
                                                 (application)
```

```
    {
            MEP = In-Out;
            requires = {das.validate,das.update};
    }

    operation confirm cancel(application):invalidApplication(application)
    {
            MEP = In-Out;
            requires = {das.validate,das.update};
    }

    operation confirm reject( application )
    {
            MEP = Out-In;

    }

    query application[0..n] get() : invalidQuery();

    event newApplication(application)
    {
            MEP = Out;
            application.lifecycle.state = created;
    }


    event applicationCanceled(application)
    {
            MEP = Out;
            application.lifecycle.state = canceled;
    }

    event offerAccepted(application)
    {
            MEP = Out;
            application.lifecycle.state = accepted;
    }

    event offerAccepted(application.offer)
    {
                MEP = Out;
    }

    fault invalidApplication(application)
    {

    }
}


public interface scheduler
{
    operation meeting scheduleInterview( meeting ) :
                            invalidMeetingRequest(meeting)
    {
            MEP = Out-In;
    }

    fault invalidMeetingNotice(meeting)
    {
        }
}
```

```
public interface background
{
  operation background check(background) : invalidBackground(background),
                        backgroundDoesNotMatch(background)
  {
       MEP = Out-In;
  }

  fault invalidBackground(background)
  {
  }

  fault backgroundDoesNotMatch(background)
  {
  }
}

public interface employee
{

  operation application processApplicationReview( application ) :
                              invalidApplication(application)
  {
       MEP = In-Out;
  }

  operation confirm processReview(application) :
                                  invalidReview(application)
  {
       MEP = In-Out;
       requires = {das.validate, das.update};
           }

  operation confirm processOffer( application ) :
                                  invalidOffer(application)
  {
        MEP = In-Out;
        requires = {das.validate, das.update};
  }

  operation confirm rejectCandidate( application ) :
                              invalidApplication(application)
  {
       MEP = In-Out;
       requires = {das.validate, das.update};
  }


  operation confirm hireApplicant(application) :
                              invalidCandidate(application)
  {
       MEP = Out-In;
  }

  fault invalidReview()
  {
  }

  fault invalidCandidate(application)
  {
  }
```

```
    fault invalidOffer(application)
    {
    }

    fault invalidApplication(application)
    {
    }

}

private interface das()
{
  operation application create(application) :
                          invalidApplication(application)
    {
        MEP = Out-In;
    }

  operation application update(application) :
                          invalidApplication(application)
    {
        MEP = Out-In;
    }

  operation application markDelete(application) :
                          invalidApplication(application)
    {
        MEP = Out-In;
    }

  operation application archive(application) :
                          invalidApplication(application)
    {
        MEP = Out-In;
    }

  query application[0..n] get()
    {
        MEP = Out-In;
    }

  fault invalidApplication(application)
    {
    }
}
//Service Implementation goes here
}
}
```

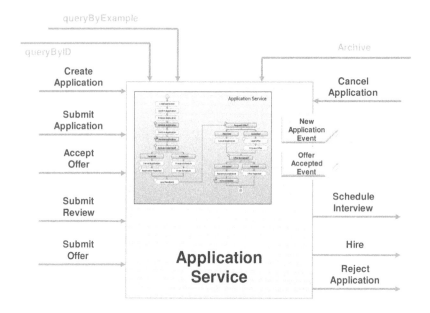

Figure 39. Some of the operations of the application service surface

Implementation

Wsper's programming language is state based. States are explicit constructs of the language and are used to control the flow of messages. Paradoxically, state management has been totally ignored by mainstream programming languages, yet this is possibly the hardest code to write, debug and change. This is especially true when the state has to be persisted over long periods of time. State management is also critical when dealing with concurrency[74].

This is yet another difference between Object Orientation and Service Orientation in the context of dealing with concurrency. I would like to encourage you to read this reference74 from V. Akhmechet which offers a refreshing view on concurrency and object orientation using message passing.

This is the implementation of the Application Service using wsper. It is using the on(state) construct which is enabled when the resource is in a particular state. As the service implementation receives messages the code can change the state in which the resource is.

```
implementation
{
   application app << receive(application.create,yes)
   {
      //validate & update are invoked automatically;
      //In case application is invalid, we return to the point
      //where we are waiting to receive the request
      retry = true; //retry is true by default
      app.lifecycle.state is created;
   } reply >> confirm(app) || invalidApplication(app);

   on (app.lifecycle.state is created)
   {
      xor flow
      {
         repeat
         {
            app << receive(application.update)
            {
            } reply >> confirm(app) || invalidApplication(app);
         } until (app.lifecycle.state != created);
         app << receive(application.process)
         {
            app.lifecycle.state is submitted;

         } reply >> confirm(app) || invalidApplication(app);
         app << receive(application.cancel)
         {
            app.lifecycle.state is canceled;
         } reply >> confirm(app) || invalidApplication(app);
      }
   }

   on (app.lifecycle.state is submitted)
   {
      xor flow
      {
         app << receive(application.process)
         {
            app.lifecycle.state is reviewed;
         } reply >> confirm(app) ;
         app << receive(application.cancel)
         {
            app.lifecycle.state is canceled;
         } reply >> confirm(app) || invalidApplication(app);
      }
   }


   on(app.lifecycle.state is reviewed)
   {
      or flow
      {
         app << receive(application.reject)
         {
            app.lifecycle.state is rejected;

         } reply >> confirm(app) ;
         app << receive(application.process)
         {
            try
            {
```

```
                    app || backgroundDoesNotMatch(app) <<
                            invoke(background.check) >> app;

            foreach( interviewer in app.reviewer)
            {
                app << invoke(scheduler.scheduleInterview)>>
                                                        app;
            }
            confirm(app) << invoke( das.update ) >> app;
            app.lifecycle.state is
                        interviewScheduled;
        } catch( backgroundDoesNotMatch(app))
        {
            app.lifecycle.state is rejected;
        }
    } reply >> confirm(app) ;
    app << receive(application.cancel)
    {
        app.lifecycle.state is canceled;
    } reply >> confirm(app) || invalidApplication(app);

    }
}

on(app.lifecycle.state is interviewScheduled) {
  or flow
  {
    forany( interviewer in app.reviewer)
      {
        app << receive(employee.processReview(app))
        {

        } reply >> confirm(app) | invalidApplication(app);
      }
    app << receive(application.cancel)
    {
        app.lifecycle.state is canceled;
    } reply >> confirm(app) || invalidApplication(app);
    app << receive(employee.rejectCandidate)
    {
        app.lifecycle.state is rejected;
    } reply >> confirm(app) || invalidApplication(app);
    app << receive(employee.processOffer)
    {
        app << invoke(application.offer) >> app;
        app.lifecycle.state is offered;
    } reply >> confirm(app) || invalidApplication(app);
  }
}


on(app.lifecycle.state is offered)
{
  xor flow
  {
    app << receive(application.acceptOffer)
    {
        app.lifecycle.state is accepted;
    } reply >> confirm(app) || invalidApplication(app);
    app << receive(application.cancel)
    {
        app.lifecycle.state is refused;
```

```
            } reply >> confirm(app) || invalidApplication(app);

    }
}


on(app.lifecycle.state is accepted)
{
    confirm(app) << invoke(employee.hireApplicant) >>
                                        app.candidate;
    app.lifecycle.state is hired;
}

on(app.lifecycle.state in {canceled,rejected,refused})
{
    terminate();
}
}
```

Component and Assembly definitions

We define here an application component as being a composition between
the application and the scheduler service.

```
component application composes application, scheduler
{
    public interface application;
    public interface employee
    public interface background

    connector(application.scheduleInterview,schedule.schedule
Meeting)
    {
        //The map can be defined programmatically
        //or later at deployment time.
        map(application,meeting)                      =
file("/wsper/demo/hr/application/app_mee.xslt");
    }
}
```

The Job Application assembly is represented Figure 40 and the wsper's
assembly definition is features on the next page.

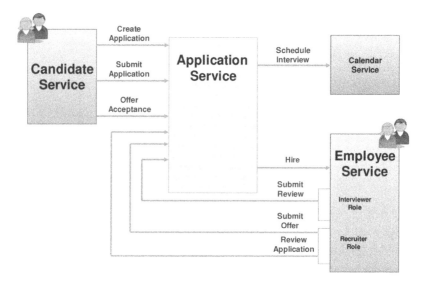

Figure 40. Representation of the Job Application Assembly

```
package org.wsper.demo.hr.assembly
{
    uses {
        package org.wsper.demo.hr.application;
        package org.wsper.demo.hr.candidate;
        package org.wsper.demo.util;
    }

assembly
{
    component application;

    component candidate implements candidate

    component employee implements employee, recruiter, interviewer
    {
        public restricted interface employee
        {
            operation hire( person, employee);
        }

        public interface recruiter;
        public interface interviewer;
    }

    //Canditate -> Application
    connector(candidate.createApplication,application.createAppli
                                                        cation);
    connector(candidate.updateApplication,application.updateAppli
                                                        cation);
    connector(candidate.submitApplication,application.submitAppli
                                                        cation);
    connector(candidate.createApplication,application.createAppli
                                                        cation);
```

```
connector(candidate.cancelApplication,application.cancelAppli
                                            cation);
connector(candidate.searchApplication,application.getApplication);

//Application -> Employee
connector(employee.createInterviewReport,application.reviewAppli
                                            cation);
connector(employee.submitInterviewReport,application.createAppli
                                            cation);
connector(employee.reviewApplication,application.reviewAppli
                                            cation);
connector(employee.updateInterviewReport,application.createAppli
                                            cation);
connector(employee.applicationCanceled,application.appli
                                        cationCanceled);

connector(employee.hire,application.hireApplicant);

}

}
```

WSPER and Process Orientation

So far the Job Application business process definition is not explicitly apparent in wsper. This is because wsper does not yet enable the specification of business process definitions. The initial work focused on getting service implementation right on the foundation of a stateful orchestration language. The working group will investigate later whether business process definitions can be implemented readily with the language or if they require specific constructs. It has long been believed that there is an isomorphic relationship between business process metamodels and orchestration languages. Personally, I am not yet convinced this is true. The main problem I see is that the proposed approach does not create a separation between business entity services and the process definition. Instead, it requires creating an overall orchestration definition that includes the process definition and all the business entity services that participate in the process. This is not necessarily a good coupling. IBM is, to the best of my knowledge, the furthest advanced in this area[75]. However there is not yet and official transformation between BPMN[76] and BPEL.

Figure 41 represents a potential view of the Job Application process based on the BPMN notation. It has been simplified and does not features an exception path other than the application could be rejected after the review by the recruiter or after the interview. It does not account for timeouts or cancellations. The offer cannot be refused either.

What is striking is that the Application Service and the Application events are not apparent in the process definition while the boundaries of the solution human tasks (in blue) do not match precisely the activities defined in the process. Process definitions typically represent the point of view of user(s) performing activities. This point of view and their underlying units of work rarely reflect how a system is used or even constructed. Actually, over time, processes change but systems rarely do. The outcome of the system(s) is to make sure that this process executes as specified. In most cases, you should expect having a developer translating process definitions into user tasks, service invocations and service interactions. The automation of this development task is still in heavy research mode and is not critical to start building composite solutions.

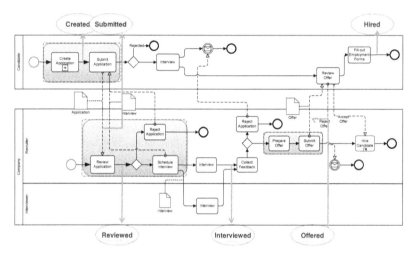

Figure 41. Job Application Business Process In Relation to Tasks, Events and Services

WSPER's Architecture

Wsper's goal is to create an application model where business logic can be captured in platform independent artifacts.

Wsper's application model aims at being implemented on top of existing Service Oriented Infrastructures (SOI). A wsper implementation is typically a compiler which compiles the platform independent artifacts into platform specific artifacts. This compiler would typically embed the best practices that are defined today around XML Schema, WSDL or BPEL design. This approach should lower dramatically the barrier of entry for new developers. I do not believe that the barrier of entry should be brought down to the level of Object Orientation. Sure, it is great to be able to expose some methods of a class as service operations, but forcing the development of composite solutions to adopt this model is a recipe for disaster. On the other hand of the spectrum, letting developers loose with the thousands of pages of SOA specifications is also a recipe for disaster even if they are taught best practices to avoid some of the pitfalls.

Wsper aims at being syntax independent and all syntaxes produced to write wsper artifacts should be produced from wsper's metamodel, i.e. be isomorphic from each other.

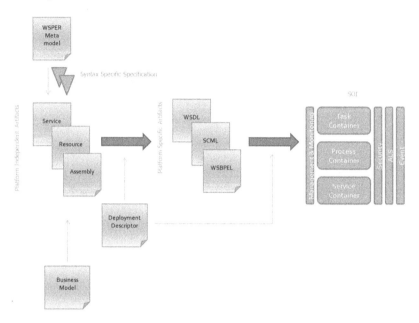

Figure 42. Wsper's Architecture.

7

Designing Services for Reuse

In this section, we are going to explore some of the design consideration for identifying and creating reusable services. The literature is full of recommendations on the topic, but the one that stood out for me was the comprehensive SAP Enterprise Service Design Guide[77] with a detailed list of service identification indicators.

I am going to focus on services that can help improve user productivity and enterprise services which can be harvested by service enabling existing service of records. I will also provide a series of recommendation on message type design, operations (with a focus on message exchange patterns) and finally I will introduce the notion of a business envelope as an important design pattern for SOA and composite solutions.

A good starting point when you try to get your hands around the service concept is to take look at physical services that you use day to day are a great analogy to think about service oriented design. At the post office for instance when we mail a letter, we exercise some of the key concepts of service orientation:

- *Context independence* – you don't pay a different price if you mail an invoice, an order, a simple letter, … i.e. the post office doesn't know anything about the context in which you mail a document. The more context independent you are, the more likely you will be able to expand the number of consumers
- *Quality of Service* – A service may offer different QoS: express, air mail, registered, return receipt… Each quality of service may open up different consumer opportunities
- *Service composition* – New services can be offered on top of a shipping service (e.g. mail order, imagine if every widget company had to create and operate their own shipping service).
- *Abstraction* – We don't know how the service is implemented (collection, …). After all, you don't have to call for pick up, reserve trucks, plains and mailmen do deliver a letter !

- *No need for integration* – No need to go through a complex customer integration to ship a letter. It is your choice to provide a return address, that's as far as customer integration goes.
- *Availability* – It is there no matter what (and no need to reserve its usage,…)

At the information system level, service orientation aims at creating abstractions of existing systems of records that in turn will be composed into new solutions. For instance you can think of wanting to have a "Document Management Service" rather than a "Document Management System". With a service interface, most processes and existing applications can leverage document centric functionality rather than forcing users to use two systems to perform a single task (an application and document management system).

Improving User Productivity

When trying to identify new services, a good lead is to look for user inefficiencies. How many applications are necessary to perform tasks within your organization? The answer is likely to be several (internal or external) applications per task. This leads to higher training cost, data quality issues, poor morale… In a composite programming model the task engine enables users to invoke any service from a particular task, in essence achieving a first level of federation, directly at the presentation layer.

Figure 43 looks back at our Job Application example from section 5 and list a series of services that can be invoked from the recruiter task reviewing the application to decide whether to invite this candidate for an interview or not:

- A Google search service would be invoked automatically from the task (as a pre-action) and display the results for a search on the candidate name and phone number for instance

- An ADP[78] background check could also be requested by the recruiter after reviewing the resume (or automatically as a post-action of the task if the outcome is positive)

- An Outlook scheduling service could also be invoked by the recruiter once he or she has selected the interviewers. The goal of this service is to schedule interviews. Once Outlook has found the ideal schedule, it will invoke the webex service that sets up a webex session if some attendees are remote

- After the phone screening interviews are complete, the recruiter should be able to invoke an Expedia service which based on the location of the candidate and the day of the interview will schedule the candidate trip

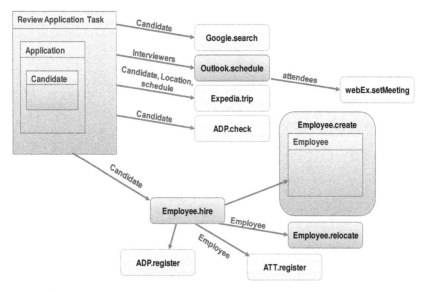

Figure 43. Services invoked from the presentation layer augment user productivity

This trend has already started outside a formal traditional programming model. Mashups[79,80,81] have become extremely popular and bring heterogeneous functionality into a single point of usage.

Normalized interactions

Services are also a great concept to implement normalized interaction with information system. Most business objects within an organization span multiple systems. When a given solution needs to update, say some customer properties, it has to update multiple systems (Figure 44). In a traditional application model, the solution will update a system of record (or several systems of record) and the changes will percolate to others via an EAI backbone.

A large class of services should be designed as a façade to the enterprise's systems of record. Over time, this gives a much better chance to retire one or more of those systems.

This pattern combined with a composite application model provides a great benefit and introduces a couple of issues. The tremendous benefit is that the business process context is no longer coupled to the business object system of record. In a traditional model, there is only one data store and this context is often implemented by sharing the same tables as the business object itself. The system of record is left with the management of the state(s) of the business object instances, guided by its intrinsic state machine (independent of any business process). This coupling alone could be responsible for 50-60% of the inefficiencies associated to information system construction.

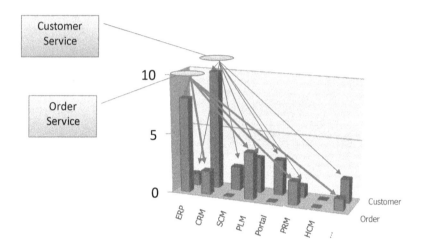

Figure 44. Service Interfaces as Normalized Interactions with Systems of Record

The normalized interaction pattern introduces a couple of issues though. First and foremost is the management of relationships between the business objects. Data is relational in nature, there is nothing we can do about it. This statement compromises the principle of autonomy of the services. When I call the "getOrderByNumber" operation of the Purchase Order service, how does the service provide customer or product information as part of the order (Figure 45)? Does it invoke a customer service before returning the order data? Does it cache this information? Does it tap directly in the customer systems of record within its implementation? Does it push the responsibility further to get that data? Is it using a Just-In-Time replication mechanism? Well the answer is probably, all of the above, depending on the performance and scalability that you are looking for. The ER model supports[82] only one type of relationship based on the primary key-foreign key mechanism. From there, two types of navigable relationships can be derived (1-to-many and many-to-many). However these logical types do not make particular distinctions between the different types of containment relations: aggregation and composition.

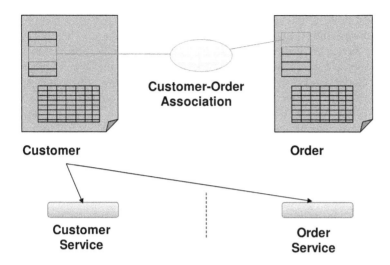

Figure 45. The Customer-Order relationship

It is recommended to choose a coarse granularity when it comes to business entity services such as the one we used for the Application business object in section 5 which contains application, candidate, and position information. If we go back to our job application example from the last section, there is no particular reason to create an application service and a candidate service because they both have roughly the same lifecycle (Figure 46). When the candidate is hired, the application's candidate information is projected to the employee service.

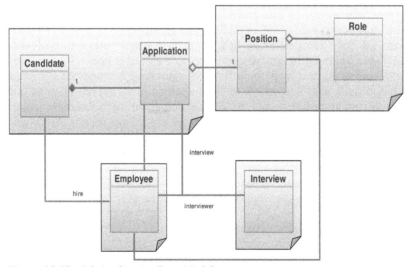

Figure 46. The Job Application Data Model

The second issue is the related to the elements that make up a business object data structure (Figure 47). In object orientation there is no specific distinction between identity, content and state, it is the responsibility of the developer to know whether this property represents the object identity or not, or understand in which state the object is). On the other hand, ER clearly identifies the concept of identify since it is an essential constituent to realize relationships. Because OO was designed for a "closed process" environment it was thought to be an advantage to hide the notion of identity to the developer.

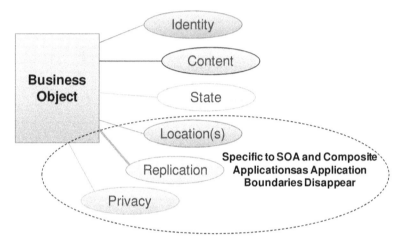

Figure 47. Elements of a business object in a service oriented architecture

In a connected world, identity is crucial to find a record or decide whether two records are really one and the same. Similarly, OO and ER do not make the concept of state explicit. The developer is left to constantly create ad hoc state machines. In a connected system the notion of state and state alignment is critical compared to a closed process, where states are of course aligned by default. But that's not it, in a connected system, a resource must also keep track of the locations of its representations and the replication policies, and of course consumer of a business object record must have an idea of the location of the master record. Automatic notification and/or replications should be triggered to the different locations in case its state changes. Finally, a resource definition should allow for privacy policies such that the consumers of the information have an indication either at the resource type or resource instance levels of how they should share the information they just consumed.

Business Entity lifecycles

Another type of service is the one that manages business object lifecycle (which itself almost always need to implement the normalized interaction pattern). In our example this corresponds to the Job Application Service

(Figure 48). The implementation is typically in WS-BPEL and manages all the interaction with human tasks and the systems of records.

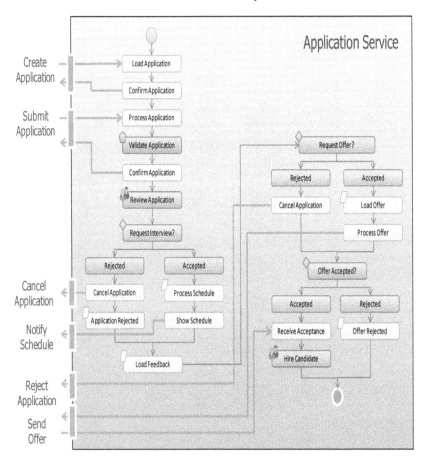

Figure 48. Job Application Service Implementation (Pseudo BPEL notation)

CRUD Operations

CRUD operations are typically implemented with the Normalized Interaction pattern. Except for queries, they are rarely exposed as is to a service consumer. Generally the CRUD operation consumers are the business entity lifecycle services.

They often need to consume the identity of the principal which is currently requesting the create, update or delete.

- ***Create*** – They are usually associated to the lifecycle of the business entity so they would extremely rarely be independent operations

- *Read* – Business entities need to be retrieved
  - Query by IDs, often in relation to work items or navigation
  - Query by examples to find a particular business entity instance (and its lifecycle)
- *Update* – Operations that update the state of an object (and trigger a state transition) are associated to the business entity lifecycle operations. Operations that purely update the content of the business entity may be independent operations
- *Delete* – Pure "delete" operations are extremely rare in business, Often closes the lifecycle of a business entity (its state cannot be changed)
  - Marked delete
  - Ready for archiving

Events

An event represents the occurrence of a given "state". In the job application example, states include:

- Application submitted
- Application rejected
- Offer Accepted

Potentially all state transitions will lead to an event. I'd like to make the point again that in reality, there is no difference between Service Oriented Architecture and Event Driven Architecture[83], they are part of the same programming model.

In general it is not necessary to publish all possible events, only the one that are relevant to the business should be published. Events enable even looser coupling mechanisms because independent business processes may be triggered by an event. Otherwise we would have to specify a single business process encompassing several subprocess definitions, making it hard to change and maintain. However the use of events makes it just a "tiny bit" more difficult to understand the overall behavior of the system

Decisions

Business rules engines have established themselves as a major piece of IT infrastructure of the last 15 years. Their role is likely to increase as part of a new discipline within IT: Enterprise Decision Management[84]. Complex and critical decision points within a task, process or business object should be externalized (and reused as part of a normalization process) as much as possible.

Service Enablement

Existing or new resources can be exposed as services following this service enablement architecture (Figure 49).

Service invocation is usually wrapped in both a technical envelope (SOAP) which enables the secure, reliable, transactional message exchange and a business envelope which provide context to the request. If you were to service enable a resource, you would need:

- An endpoint to listen on incoming messages (a service can expose multiple endpoints, listening on different transports)
- An activation framework that decides how to process a request from a threading perspective
- A security framework that decides whether the request is authenticated and authorized and perform decryption services
- A context management service which performs correlation and dehydration/hydration services
- A Quality of Service facility which monitors requests, responses and resources
- A connection management facility to deal with connectivity to resources: RDBMS, existing systems, or other services (web services, SCA,…)

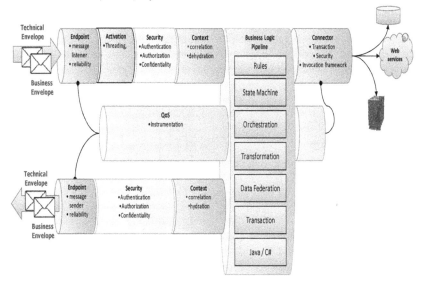

Figure 49. Service Enablement Architecture

You may not be familiar with the concept of hydration (and dehydration). This is a fancy term, part of the WS-BPEL jargon, that relates to the fact that when a process instance is inactive for some time, the process engine usually "dehydrates" the instance by storing it on a permanent media (rather than keeping it in memory for extended periods of time, days, weeks…). Hydration is the opposite and consists at retrieving the process instance when a message correlated to it is received.

The business logic itself can potentially be expressed in many different ways and any combination of (Figure 50):

- Traditional programming languages: Java, C#, … this is mostly used to simple request processes
- Orchestration (WS-BPEL) or state machines, which are used for composite services and the implementation of services that involve a long running sequence of operation
- Transformation: to translate an incoming request in a format understandable by the resource
- Data federation (EII): when multiple resources need to be invoked to perform the service
- Transaction logic: to compensate for failure
- Rules and Decisions: for routing purposes for instance
- …

A service container offers all these capabilities more or less packaged with a set of tools to facilitate the enablement process, the deployment and minimize the dependencies of the business logic on all the other aspects of the service (security, transaction, reliability,…)

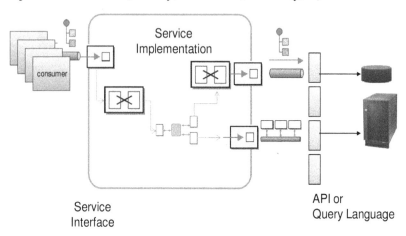

Figure 50. A Typical service implementation

Business Entity Schema Design Guidelines

There are several XML Schema Design Patterns approaches for schema design[85],[86]:

- Venetian Blind
- Garden of Eden
- Hybrid (Venetian Eden)

In the Venetian Blind pattern, all global-level components in a schema are defined as a type except the root. The Garden of Eden pattern in addition requires that all elements must be defined globally.

The open applications group recommends[87] using the Hybrid XML Schema Design Pattern which is based on the following key principles:

1. *Global types and elements are used to represent reusable constructs that have sufficient semantics independent of the context in which they are used.*

2. *Local types and elements are used to represent constructs that are only meaningful within a specific context.*

3. *All classes are expressed as complexTypes in the XML Schema.*

4. *All attributes of a class are declared as local xsd:element within the corresponding xsd:complexType.*

5. *Classes associated through aggregation (e.g. Party, BuyerParty) are globally declared as an xsd:element and referenced in the aggregating element.*

6. *Classes associated through composition (e.g. PurchaseOrderHeader and PurchaseOrderLine) are locally declared as xsd:element elements within the xsd:complexType of the PurchaseOrder. A Composition ASBIE is defined as a specialized type of ASBIE that represents a composition relationship between the associating ABIE and the associated ABIE.*

7. *Generalization associations indicate classes that inherit the source class. This is represented in XML Schema using complexType derivation by extension.*

This pattern supports well data binding strategies at the presentation and data level layers.

This is typically the kind of concepts which can be implemented behind an abstract framework such as wsper from a business object definition. No one should have to deal with the intricacies of XML Schema. XML Schema is well designed, but is we extend David Chappell's train of thought on WS-BPEL, this is again at the byte code level.

Loose coupling is not just about using a common syntax and protocols, it is also about creating and managing a set of shared semantics. A schema design architecture would be useless if every schema designer could use, invent and reinvent its own semantics at will. Dave Linthicum provided a set of recommendations[88] on service construction centered on the idea of the using abstraction layer vs. a common information model, materialized by "shared schemas" across service interfaces:

1. *You need to face the data first and define a common data or abstraction layer so that the services are not bound to a particular schema, but enjoy the use of the data nonetheless. I would not push a common schema as much as an abstraction layer.*

2. *The abstracted or common model should be tested like any other component.*

3. *Don't focus as much on force fitting a data model as agreement across the service domains, and leverage a schema mapping layer to provide choices in the future and agility down at the data layer*

David's experience shows that relying on a common set of schemas may prove to be inflexible when designing service interfaces because it will prevent these services to evolve separately.

It would be naïve to think that consumers will always be in the position to adopt the point of view of the provider or that both the provider and the consumer can always adopt the same point of view. Even if this were true today, overtime, the consumer and provider may not be in the position to evolve at the same time towards a newer version of the interface.

Even though mediation is not explicit in the W3C's web service architecture[89], SOA practitioners have long ago used it systematically to achieve a higher level of loose coupling and enable separate evolutions between the consumers and providers. Whichever mediation mechanism you use: publish/subscribe, orchestration, polymorphic interface... it will always result in using transformations from the consumer schema to the provider schema and back. These transformations may be performed by a coordinator or on premises in the consumer or provider service container.

Since these transformations are inevitable, the question becomes, how can you minimize their impact at design-time and run-time? Incidentally, if you were to use a common information model independent of the provider and consumer interface and still want to achieve loose coupling, you would incur the cost of two transformations, not to mention that you still need to transform your message format into a data set consumable by the implementation of the provider and consumer.

The first steps towards more manageable transformations, is to capture the semantics of the information contained in your messages and derive consumer and provider interfaces from these semantics. This is what Dave calls an "abstraction layer" or others call a canonical data model[90] or an ontology. In this abstraction layer, the structure is less important than the normalization of the semantics. This problem is not new, David Webber[91], way back in 1998 had introduced the concept of bizcodes, to normalize diverging names XML formats and deal elegantly with localization. More recently, the UN/CEFACT has developed a set of standards to help with the management of semantics and data format: the Core Component Technical Specification[92,93]; one of the concepts being the notion of "context" whereby you can manage the common parts of a schema across 8 dimensions (for instance, it helps manage the commonality between a purchase order in the automotive industry in Germany and a purchase order in the semi-conductor industry in the USA).

Semantics have to be managed precisely under strict governance processes and tested. Traceability to physical artifacts such as a service interface definitions or a database schemas is key to develop a successful ontology.

Service Operation Design Guidelines

Each interface to a service describes one or more service operations that can be performed by the service. For extremely simple services, there may only be one operation. Most services have several operations. Enterprise services are often a gateway to functionality provided by existing systems. Their granularity and the operations they can expose depend heavily on the systems of record they encapsulate.

The most important design rule in a Service Oriented Architecture is to create operations that can participate in as many business processes as possible. Actually, this simple rule epitomizes the main difference between EAI and SOA: even though web-services can be created from an integration API, these APIs most often expose the points at which the process(es) need to be synchronized with the one of other applications. This leaves a large class of potentially reusable services embedded with the system itself inaccessible via this process synchronization API.

One of the key consideration when designing an operation is the choice of the message exchange patterns which implements the operation. In the following three sub-sections we will review the WSDL 2.0 message patterns (MEPs), the transactional MEPs from the WS-TX specification and the business MEPs from the ebBP specification.

Message Exchange Patterns

WSDL 2.0[94] was designed with an extensible set of message exchange patterns as opposed to WSDL 1.1. which only supports a fixed set. The MEPs model typical message exchanges between software agents from the point of view of the server (the first agent which receives a message). They specify the direction, sequencing and cardinality of the messages. MEPs can be specified between any number of nodes, not just two. In practice I have not seen people defining their own MEPs but this is definitely a direction people will go since it will improve the reusability of complex services.

Examples of WSDL 2.0 MEPs[95,96] can be found in the table below.

Pattern/Criteria	Short Description
In-only	Exactly one message received from a node in the "In" direction. This pattern uses no fault rule.
Robust In-Only	Exactly one message received from a node in the "In" direction. This pattern uses a Message Triggers Fault rule.
In-Out	Exactly two messages, in order, received by a node where the direction is "In" and sent by the same node where direction is "Out". This pattern uses a Fault Replace Message rule.
In-Optional-Out	One or two messages, in order, received from some node in the "In" direction and optionally sent by the same node in the "Out" direction. The pattern uses a Message Triggers Fault rule.
Out-Only	Exactly one message sent to a node in the "Out" direction. This pattern uses no fault rule.

Robust Out-Only	Exactly one message sent to a node in the "Out" direction. This pattern uses a Message Triggers Fault rule.
Out-In	Exactly two messages, in order, sent to a node where the direction is "Out" and received from the same node where direction is "in". This pattern uses a Fault Replace Message rule.
Out-Optional-in	One or two messages, in order, sent from some node in the "Out" direction and optionally received by the same node in the "In" direction. The pattern uses a Message Triggers Fault rule.

Fault rules

For each message, WSDL 2.0 specifies three possible fault rules:

Fault Replaces Message

Any message after the first in the pattern MAY be replaced with a fault message, which MUST have identical cardinality and direction. The fault message MUST be delivered to the same target node as the message it replaces.

Message Triggers Fault

Any message, including the first one, MAY trigger a fault message in response. Each recipient MAY generate a fault message, and MUST generate no more than one fault for each triggering message. Each fault message has direction the reverse of its triggering message. The fault message MUST be delivered to the originator of the message which triggered it. If there is no path to this node, the fault MUST be discarded.

No Faults

No faults may be generated.

Transactional Message Exchange Patterns

Transaction protocols represent the message interchange between the transaction coordinator and transaction participants. The three distributed transaction protocol categories are[97]:

- **Provisional-Final**: do the application work but mark it as provisional. If told to confirm, mark the provisional work as final. If told to cancel, delete the provisional work or mark it cancelled.

- **ACID** is just a version of Provisional-Final where the Provisional effects are invisible.
  - o Provisional effects in a business transaction may be made visible.
  - o The ACID Isolation requirement does imply locking, which is not suitable for long-running transactions or those involving autonomous participants.
- **Validate-Do**: validate that the application work could be done, and do it if told to confirm. If told to cancel, no application work has been done anyway.
- **Do-Compensate**: immediately do the application work as if it is final, and later undo if told to cancel. If told to confirm, the application work has already been done.

A transaction protocol can be decomposed in two elements:

- A state alignment protocol
- A transaction scenario

One of the key requirements of a transaction protocol is that the state between the coordinator and all the participants be aligned, even when messages cannot be exchanged via the utilization of timeouts.

A state alignment protocol is mandatory to monitor the execution of actions. It specifies a message exchange pattern between the two parties exchanging requests for action. In order to guarantee state alignment, all requests for action must be followed by a status notification indicating where the processing of the action of successful or failed.

A state alignment protocol is reusable across any number of requests for action and should contain:

- One or more Message exchange patterns (In, In-Out,…)
- One or more signals (confirm) and their signification (success, failure, types of failures,…)
- Timeouts if appropriate (may be overridden by the transaction scenario specification)
- Transport quality of service (QoS) (e.g. Reliable Delivery)

A state alignment protocol can be used to specify transaction scenarios, decoupling in essence the scenario specification from the need to always achieve state alignment.

A transaction scenario will specify which patterns are used to send the protocol specific requests for action or status notifications. In some cases, the signals are also specified at this level as a configuration of the template though it is not a recommended practice.

To minimize the number of messages exchanges, you may combine the state alignment protocol with the transaction scenario. This is what WS-TX has done with the WS-AtomicTransaction protocol which is aligned with a two phase commit protocol:

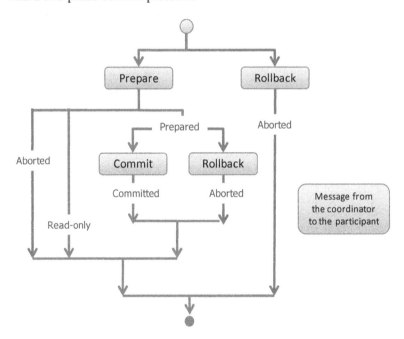

Figure 51 WS-AT 2PC Transaction Scenario

This transaction scenario[98] is composed of three requests for action (Figure 51) all sent by the coordinator to participants: Prepare, Commit and Rollback, all implemented using a notification. The participant may respond to these notifications with different signals (prepared, committed, aborted, read only). If you look at the state machine of this protocol, you will see that at any moment in time the state of the transaction is perfectly known to the participants and coordinator.

Operation Business Patterns

In a composite solution, every operation should be annotated with one of the following business operations[99]:

Pattern/Criteria	Short Description	Example Use Case
Notification	A formal information exchange between parties.	A seller notify its buyer of an incoming shipment by sending an Advance Ship Notice (ASN).
Information Distribution	An informal information exchange between parties	A Seller notifies its Buyers of the release of a new product line that become part of an product catalog. As each Buyer retains a copy of the product catalog, they may acknowledge receipt. Without non-repudiation, Information Distribution may be difficult to prove authorship and adherence.
Request-Response	A request and response where no residual obligation is created (for example, a request for price and availability). The request/response activity pattern shall be used for interactions when a consumer requests information that a service provider already has and when the request for information requires a complex interdependent set of results.	A Buyer asks a Seller in a request for the price and availability of a particular product. This request does not result in the responding party allocating product for future purchase. The Seller queries its inventory and other applications to provide a sufficient response by checking their Supply Chain Management and Inventory systems. The Seller has to calculate the current price based on availability, its Suppliers' details, etc. Most often, the Request-Response does not involve a simple Yes/No answer from the responding party.

Request-Confirm	Used where a service consumer requests confirmation about its status with respect to previous conversations or a provider's business rules.	A Buyer requests from a Seller if it is still authorized to sell certain product. The Buyer expects a confirmation response. A response does not equate to an obligation, although further action could subsequently occur. A previous contract may or may not have existed between the parties. The Seller confirms he is still authorized to sell the product. Typically, the Request-Confirm involves a simple Yes/No answer from the responding party.
Query Response	Used by a service consumer for an information query that service provider already has.	A Buyer asks a Seller in a request for the price and availability of a particular product. This request does not result in the responding party allocating product for future purchase. The Seller maintains a online product catalog of products and can provide the Buyer a response without complex constraints or backend processing.
Transaction	Formal obligation between the service consumer and provider	A buyer requests a product or service in a specific time delivered to a pre-determined location from a Seller. Accepting the obligation, the Seller agrees and commits to delivery to complete a business transaction. The parties may have a pre-existing agreement to exchange goods and payment.

These business operation types will be implemented with similar transaction and MEPs and will lead to similar exception handling. Overtime it would be possible to automate some aspect of the service definition and implementation.

Message type Schema Design Guidelines

Another aspect of operation design is of course the design of the operation message types. There have been long discussions on the merits of operation schema design ever since SOAP and WSDL were published.[100] It looks like the industry has standardized on the wrapped document-literal pattern which consists of a root element that name the operation (since WS-I Basic Profile forbids the utilization of the SOAP action to identify an operation) and the sub elements contains the payload of the message.

My recommendation is to construct each message with a business envelope that follows some of the guidelines of the Open Applications Group's Business Object Document (BOD) architecture[101] by using:

- **A BOD** Envelope – identifies the Verb, Noun, revision and runtime environment (Test or Production in which the BOD instance is to be used.). The BOD is comprised of :
    - o *An Application Area* – communicates information that can be used by the infrastructure to communicate the message.
    - o *A Data Area* –carries the business specific payload or data communicated by the BOD.
- **Verbs** – Verb identifies the action being performed on the specific Noun of the BOD.
- **Nouns** – identify the business specific data that is being communicated (i.e. PurchaseOrder, SalesOrder, Quote, Route, Shipment, etc.) They are comprised of Components, which are described below.
    - o *Components* –are extensible building blocks of a Noun. They are comprised of compounds and fields, which are described below. Components are extensible.
    - o *Compounds* – are basic, shared building blocks that are used by all BODs (i.e. Name, Address, Quantity, Amount, etc.). They are extensible through contextual use but not with additional fields (i.e. OrderedQuantity, ShippedQuantity, BackOrderedQuantity).
    - o *Fields* – are the lowest level elements defined in OAGIS. Fields are fundamental elements that are used to create Compounds and Components. (i.e. Description, Name, etc.).

The root element must be unique for every information exchange. The root element is constructed following this pattern: <VerbName><NounName>

The list of verbs used by the OAGIS is limited to the following:

- Acknowledge
- Cancel
- Change
- Confirm
- Get
- Sync
- Show
- Update
- Load
- Post
- Process
- Respond

In practice, I find it hard to limit the operations name to these verbs. There are additional semantics that I would like to convey with other verbs. Often the operation names look odd depending on the noun. However, I would really recommend managing your list of verbs to be as small as possible and stick to it because it will allow you in the future to add aspects to these types of operations. This guideline is of course inspired from the REST theory of Roy Fielding[102,103].

The nouns typically correspond to the business entity to which the operation applies.

The Open Applications Group's Application Area[101] consists of:

- *Sender* – which identifies characteristics and control identifiers that relate to the application that created the Business Object Document. The sender area can indicate the logical location of the application and/or database server, the application, and the task that was processing to create the BOD.

- *CreationDateTime* – which is the date time stamp that the given instance of the Business Object Document was created. This date must not be modified during the life of the Business Object Document

- ***BODID*** – which provides a place to carry a Globally Unique Identifier (GUID) that will make each Business Object Document instance uniquely identifiable.

The application area is typically used in combination of technical services (such as transaction logging, exception handling, re-sending, reporting…) and conveys information that is typically not found in a SOAP header.

The Data Area is where the payload of the message is carried. This is why a design such as the BOD is often referred to as a business envelope.

8

How do we start a composite software factory?

Inhibitors and risks

Inhibitors and risks are naturally associated with the adoption of such a broad concept and its enabling technologies. Every organization is different and the guidelines provided here are very general.

I recommend not to start with a large big bang enterprise architecture initiative, you need to test the waters first and get comfortable with the concepts and understand how they apply to your organization's technologies and processes. Only then, after deploying several services in production and building a few composite solutions that you would start an enterprise-wide program. A composite solution program benefits from having derived the business architecture and having a compelling set of business goals and derived the strategy to achieve them. The program, IMHO, needs to be established at the level of solution delivery. Therefore I will not address selling this type of initiative at the senior management level, because this is irrelevant. It is a mistake to think that service oriented architecture and composite solutions should be communicated and understood by senior management[104]. They are at the same level as Java EE and .Net and require a deep background to understand the far reaching implications they could potentially have on the company. How would you want them to understand how a "Customer" service is used and reused if they don't have a deep technical background? The risk is really that throwing a silver bullet could backfire if the benefits are marginal or simply did not meet the expectations of a senior manager. And, let me be clear, the benefits will be by definition marginal until you finish putting in place the new technologies and processes that are required to deliver composite solutions and of course finish training and retaining enough resources to make these projects successful. This is why you should apply the Agile principles as often as possible, "only build what you need, nothing more". The business needs results not ideas, and we technologists have a bunch of ideas.

Composite Solutions (and Service Oriented Architecture) should remain under the umbrella of your delivery organization and managed with the help of enterprise architecture, not higher. Ultimately the risk of your delivery organization not wanting to adopt this approach cannot be mitigated. If they are happy building pure Java EE or .Net based solutions and using their favorite 90s integration platform, there is no reason to deploy a Composite Solution Platform or a Service Oriented Architecture.

Technically, the main risk is the fragmentation of "the big picture" where technology choices are made tactically without achieving the degree of coherence that is needed to ensure that all aspects of the reference architecture work seamlessly together. An Agile approach need to be complemented by a precise management of the Composite Solution Platform maturity model, and guided by the projects an organization delivers. Inherently, you should be ready to accept the risk of delivery delays due to the construction of the infrastructure.

A change of this magnitude does require a senior manager champion who is going to make sure that the initiative is funded and staffed appropriately. It also requires dedicated enterprise architecture and delivery resources to help growing the knowledge of the delivery team and avoid having to train new resources all the time. Without this commitment, a composite solution platform cannot be built and solutions cannot be delivered. Initially, it is recommended to create a center of excellence to help establish a critical mass of trained resources and avoid competing with other projects for resources. Over time, the existing delivery organization should be given control of composite solution delivery.

Another important inhibitor is the impact on project ROI of the lack of trained resources, infrastructure components and business services (that could potentially be consumed in composite applications). To mitigate this risk, an organization needs to define and put in place mechanisms (as part of the governance processes for instance) by which infrastructure investments can be planned globally but triggered locally by the needs of specific projects and solutions. Projects alone cannot be held accountable for delivering infrastructure elements, shared services or even resource training.

The Composite Application Program

Figure 52 represents the major activities that are associated to the development of a Composite Solution delivery capability.

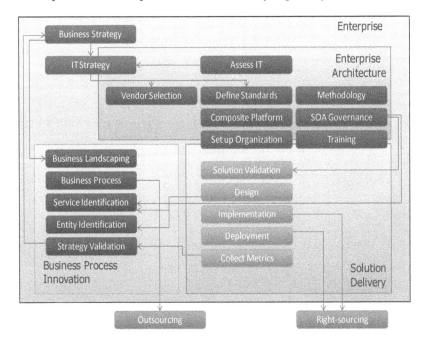

Figure 52 Establishment of a Composite Application Delivery Practice

At the top, the business and IT strategy strongly influence (and fund) the road map of the composite solution platform capabilities. They also influence which composite solutions and enterprise services are built first.

The enterprise architecture group is in charge of establishing the composite application platform, the governance council as well as defining the roles and training of the delivery teams.

Typically, a "business process innovation" group will be set up to translate the business strategy in actionable project. This group is usually mapping and refining the company's business model which includes processes, services and business entities (reference data model). This group should be staffed by modeling expert to help create assets that can be more readily consumed by delivery groups

Figure 53 represent a possible organization of composite solution delivery teams. It shows that the delivery team interacts with the service librarian to identify existing services which can be reused (with or without changes) by the solution.

If new services need to be delivered they have to go through a governance process to validate the specification of the service, identify the owner(s) of the service and its funding model.

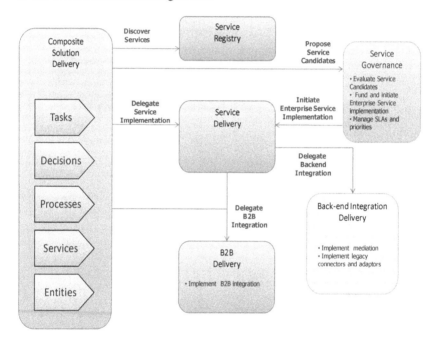

Figure 53. Composite Application Delivery Model

Because of the specialization of skills it is recommended that the service implementation team delegate B2B and back end integration to dedicated teams, possibly organized as a center of excellence. Similarly, you might already have in place an enterprise application integration team that would be responsible for the service implementation back-end connectivity, as well as any modification to the back-end systems.

Figure 54 represent the primary responsibilities of the delivery groups in the context of this proposed delivery organization. The primary owner of the service specifications should be the service delivery teams. The main reason is that the skills that are required to design good, modular and versionable message types are difficult to acquire. Over time these skills could be transferred to the solution delivery team.

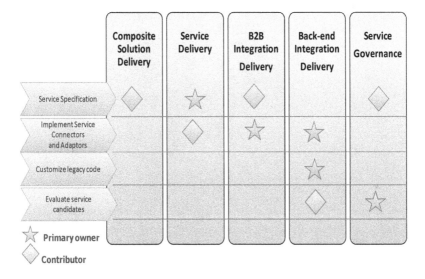

	Composite Solution Delivery	Service Delivery	B2B Integration Delivery	Back-end Integration Delivery	Service Governance
Service Specification	◇	☆	◇		◇
Implement Service Connectors and Adaptors		◇	☆	☆	
Customize legacy code				☆	
Evaluate service candidates				◇	☆

☆ Primary owner

◇ Contributor

Figure 54. Primary responsibilities of the delivery groups

Finally, Figure 55 displays the activities of the governance council at the enterprise, service and solution level. SOA governance is part of and must comply with the broad IT governance activities. SOA Governance is related to Data Governance via the entity representations embedded in operations message types. This is why a Reference Data Model (not a Common Information Model) is represented on the figure. SOA Governance should enforce the compliance of service message types with the RDM semantics.

Beyond a pure compliance role, the SOA governance[105] is driving the design, ownership and funding model of services to promote reuse. This organization should enforce that the design of a service will support the operations of potential consumers in the future. It should also help fund additional functionality that is not directly used by initial consumers but will be important for future consumers.

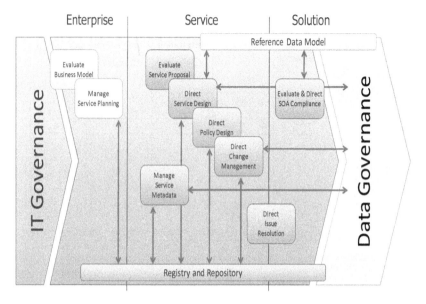

Figure 55. Governance activities at the enterprise, service and solution levels

Composite Software Maturity Model

A maturity model is typically composed of four phases[106,107,108]:

Education – IT is learning the foundational principles and technologies of Composite Applications and SOA. Learning can include experimental projects ranging from prototypes to small-scale service deployments. Note that ROI won't be recognized if you deploy during this phase; the target is not clearly defined and benefits may not be understood until after the fact.

Establishment – IT collaborates with business units and senior management. Having gathered the necessary knowledge, IT defines and builds the architecture to support current and future composite solution strategies.

Execution – By using the knowledge gained from establishing the architecture, applying lessons learned, and understanding the cost benefits to mitigate risk, IT can execute a strategy and be confident in its ability to predict outcomes.

Optimization – Having successfully executed a strategy, the technology is embraced by IT and business units. Benefits are realized, risks are managed, and Composite Solutions are part of your problem solving toolbox. At this point, senior management should be well equipped to respond to change, unconstrained by technology.

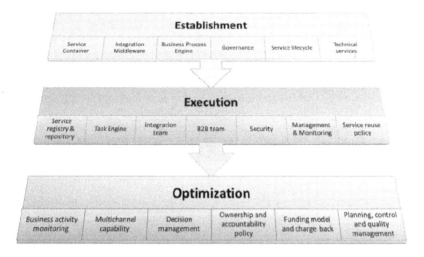

Figure 56 An example of a Technology and Organizational Maturity Model

Expected Benefits

From a business perspective, the benefits are multi-fold, even though they all sound like cliché.

Improved ROI	Reusability of assets and improve factoring of the programming model targets directly the ROI of solution delivery, either by lowering the cost of delivery or delivering more features for the same cost
Scope project for ROI	A composite application model enables to scope process automation more efficiently and focus initial development on higher ROI elements without compromising the completeness of the delivery. Such programming model is well suited to support iterative improvements as prescribed by Lean Six Sigma methodologies[109]
Time-to-market	Reusability of assets and improve factoring of the programming model reduces significantly the development cycles and improve the ability to innovate
Flexibility	The factoring of a service oriented, process centric and model driven composite programming model greatly improve the capacity to adapt and optimize solutions
Lower risks	A simplified programming model lowers the risk of not delivering the solution on time, or at all
Lower knowledge barrier	A simplified programming model lowers significantly the need to train IT staff in an otherwise heteroclite technology stack

New Buy vs Build paradigm	Today, IT is faced with build vs buy decisions which are made at the solution level. A composite programming model offers a new level of granularity and enable an IT organization to retain control over strategic aspect of the solution (processes for instance) while sourcing non core elements from third parties (system of record). An organization can now decide to buy processes, services, business object models independently.
Better factoring of the solution itself	A composite application model offers better opportunities to hand-off work back and forth with outsourcing partners, offering more options achieve optimal business models
Reuse of legacy systems	Legacy systems wrapped behind services can be reused in new solutions without the need to duplicate or change the business logic the implement
Improved consolidation capabilities	As services are often factored to expose a normalized interface to a series of legacy systems, this presents an opportunity to consolidate legacy systems without disrupting the composite solutions that leverage their business logic

From a delivery perspective we can expect that several roles will benefit from a composite programming model.

Enterprise Architect	A common programming model, defined as an abstract framework, supported by an enterprise wide implementation helps enforce the utilization of IT standards since they are usually hidden from the developers. It also help evolve these standards without breaking existing solutions
Solution Architect	Its work is not cluttered by the need to follow countless recommendations specific to a particular technology. The programming model is naturally aligned with business requirements
Business Analyst	The programming model is a lot more aligned with the formalism employed to specify requirements Operational metrics which are more naturally collected help the dialog with the business to decide the best course for the evolution of the solution
Application programmer	Developers focus on the business logic not on the intricacies of web service specifications Alleviates the need to learn a large number of standard technical services (transformation, security,...)

	The development of complex state machine to match business process definition is no longer needed. This is the part of the code that is hardest to write and QA
Quality Analyst	The factoring enables QA to focus on more manageable elements of the solution (service, process, task,…) Reused services require minimum testing A more natural path between process definition and process implementation reduces the number of defects (State Machines are the hardest elements to test)

If we look at the cost structure of delivering solution, we can expect important cost savings and quality improvements in the development area.

Typical	Delivery Costs	Changes in Total Cost of Ownership	Suggested benefit
	% of total cost		
Governance	10%	• Much lower cost of EA compliance	• 80% savings can be achieved with the use of an abstract framework like WSPER
Development	40%	• Improved communication between the business and the delivery team reduces the analysis effort • Lower design and implementation cost because of the utilization of a framework and a better alignment between programming model and requirement specifications • Lower QA costs	• 60% reduction in the requirements phase • Overall, 30% in design and implementation phases. Typically design and implementation can be lowered by 90% for business processes alone • 50% reduction
Maintenance	20%	• Solutions can be changed with much less disruption because of the factoring of the application model	• 50% reduction
Operation	30%	• The use of a single delivery infrastructure (process engine, service container, task engine,…) enables the reuse of infrastructure assets across solutions • Lower administration cost due to the standardization of the solution architecture based on a framework	• 20% reduction in license and hardware cost • 50% reduction in administration costs

These numbers can have a dramatic impact on an organization's ability to innovate. Conservatively, if we consider that the productivity of solution delivery can increase on average by a factor of 2.5 and that the budget for innovation could increase by a factor of 4 as a result of Composite Applications providing better consolidation capabilities, reuse of existing assets and lower operational costs, we can estimate that the capacity to innovate can increase by a factor of 10 (Figure 57). Again, I would not necessarily sale these numbers to senior management because they will hold you responsible for it. They are featured here to help you manage your progress and define your own metrics.

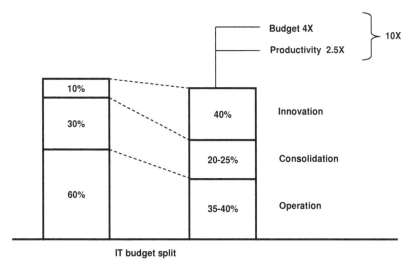

Figure 57 Impact of Composite Applications on the ability for an organization to innovate

9

Conclusion

"Business is complicated," says Jon Bosak[110] of Sun Microsystems. "Any solution that doesn't reflect that complexity is not a real solution." Information systems and their underlying infrastructure have grown to a point of extreme technical complexity making them difficult to manage, evolve, or replace deepening the divide between IT and the business. After having served as the engine behind productivity gains and new business models, information systems have now become an obstacle to innovation and change. While web applications have greatly simplified the way employees, customers, and partners access data to perform complex tasks in self-service mode, the monolithic architecture of traditional programming models keeps creating silos that cannot repurpose this information for new consumption scenarios.

After almost ten years of hard work, the Web Services specification stack is finally complete as of June 2007. Along the, way this work has spurred an unprecedented level of innovation even though its primary objective was only to achieve interoperability between otherwise incompatible programming models and technologies which had eluded past distributed computing models.

Some vendors have chosen to bolt these innovations onto their core Object Oriented runtime, while others have already started developing a sophisticated model driven, service oriented, process centric composite programming model. This programming model is bound to change dramatically the economics of IT and create new opportunities to innovate, adapt and optimize at a level never seen before. The combination of asset reuse, as well as the ability to "right-source" assets from their point of lowest operational cost will create a wide-spread adoption of composite solutions across all industries. The success of mashups at the presentation layer is just an indication of what's yet to come at the process and information layers.

This book strived to give you a new perspective on SOA, web services, programming models, model driven architecture and tools. The goal was to demonstrate that massive productivity gains can still be achieved by rationalizing the programming model of information systems and by helping developers implement business requirements more readily without transforming, hopelessly, business users into developers.

The development of composite solutions is not simple. It requires major paradigm shifts across all IT functions, the adoption of a large footprint of new technologies, new skills and a stringent discipline. This change can only happen within and with the cooperation of the delivery organization. A change of this magnitude requires new levels of abstraction. Without them, developers will be challenged by the sheer number of technologies and best practices they have to deal with in the delivery process. I sincerely hope this book will help you leverage and direct your investments in your Service Oriented Architecture and build the foundation of your Composite Solution Platform.

Jean-Jacques Dubray

Seattle, October 2007

Index

About The Author

Jean-Jacques Dubray is a SOA Enterprise Architect in a large financial institution. He started working on SOA in 1998 at NEC Systems Laboratories. Since then, he has architected three composite application frameworks at eXcelon, Eigner and Attachmate.

He has contributed to various SOA specifications as an editor of the OASIS ebXML Business Process specification and a co-author of the Service Component Architecture, Service Data Object and wsper. He has contributed to the OAGIS, BPML, WS-CAF, WS-TX and WS-CDL working groups.

He is a contributor to InfoQ.com and the creator of ebpml.org, flashreader.org and resustain.org

He earned a Ph.D. from the Faculty of Science of Luminy (Marseilles, France), home of the Prolog Programming language, where he taught an Object Oriented Programming class. He received his B.Sc. and M.Sc. from the Ecole Centrale de Lyon (Ecully, France).

He lives near Seattle where he enjoys hiking, kayaking, gardening and playing soccer or music with his kids. Even though Washington wines are quite an experience, his favourite is still a simple Patrimonio Rosé (chilled) from the island of Corsica where his family is from.

End Notes

[1] M. Ellsworth "Grid Computing Takes Off in the Enterprise", http://www.ud.com/company/news/news_2003/05012003_enterprisearchitect.pdf

[2] E. Newcomer et al "Understanding SOA with Web Services", Addison Wesley, 2006

[3] J. McGovern et al "Enterprise Service Oriented Architectures: Concepts, Challenges, Recommendations", Springer, 2006

[4] P. Herzum et al "Business Component Factory", http://www.componentfactory.org/

[5] J. Sutherland "Why I love the OMG", http://jeffsutherland.com/papers/StandardView/LoveOMG.htm

[6] T. Reenskaug, 'The Model-View-Controller (MVC) Its Past and Present', JavaZONE, Oslo, 2003, http://heim.ifi.uio.no/~trygver/2003/javazone-jaoo/MVC_pattern.pdf

[7] Dave McComb, Semantic Arts, Private Communication, 2004

[8] Nicholas Carr, "IT Doesn't Matter", republished at http://www.roughtype.com/archives/2007/01/it_doesnt_matte.php

[9] P. Herzum et al "Business Component Factory", http://www.componentfactory.org/ "

[10] J. Löwy, http://files.skyscrapr.net/users/arcast/rr/ARCastTVRR20070711-LowyWSAT.mp3

[11] R. Bosák Ostrava, "Interceptor Design Pattern ", http://dailydevelopment.blogspot.com/2007/04/interceptor-design-pattern.html

[12] David Orchard, "Guide to Versioning XML Languages using new XML Schema 1.1 features", http://www.w3.org/TR/xmlschema-guide2versioning/#openContent

[13] XLang, http://www.ebpml.org/xlang.htm

[14] BPML, http://www.ebpml.org/bpml_1_0_june_02.htm

[15] WSFL, http://www.ebpml.org/wsfl.htm

[16] WS-BPEL, http://www.eclipse.org/tptp/platform/documents/design/choreography

[17] J.J. Dubray, "WSPER: An Abstract SOA Framework", 2007, http://www.wsper.org/primer.html

[18] D. Longworth "Sending an unmistakeable message", LooselyCoupled.com http://www.looselycoupled.com/stories/2003/message-infr0528.html

[19] Sun Microsystems, "Java 2 Platform, Enterprise Edition Overview", http://java.sun.com/j2ee/appmodel.html

[20] Microsoft, ".Net Framework 3.0 Programming Model: Feature Area Overviews", http://msdn2.microsoft.com/en-us/library/ms717447.aspx

[21] Jungmin Ju, "The state-of-the-art of business process modeling and execution", Ph.D. Thesis, 2007, http://iisl.postech.ac.kr/publication/thesis/2007_jjm.pdf

[22] D. Chappell "Using the ESB Service Container",http://www.onjava.com/pub/a/onjava/excerpt/esb_ch6/index.html

[23] G. Moore's "Living on the fault line", http://www.businessweek.com/2000/00_35/b3696079.htm

[24] B. Lublinsky "Explore the role of service repositories and registries in SOA", DeveloperWorks, http://www.ibm.com/developerworks/library/ar-servrepos/index.html

[25] SCA Specifications, http://www.osoa.org/display/Main/Service+Component+Architecture+Specifications

[26] http://msdn.microsoft.com/library/default.asp?url=/library/en-us/vsent7/html/vxconDesigningForSecurability.asps

[27] B. Lublinsky "Supporting Policies in SOA",http://www.ibm.com/developerworks/webservices/library/ws-support-soa/

[28] B. Lublinsky, "Defining SOA as an architectural style",http://www.ibm.com/developerworks/library/ar-soastyle/

[29] D. Panda, "Hot deployment, How hot is it?", http://radio.weblogs.com/0135826/2004/05/17.html#a30

[30] G. Hamilton, "Multithreaded toolkits: A failed dream?", http://weblogs.java.net/blog/kgh/archive/2004/10/multithreaded_t.html

[31] M. Zahn, "Delegates and Events in C#",http://www.akadia.com/services/dotnet_delegates_and_events.html

[32] M. Boyd, "Comparing and Transforming Between Data Models via an Intermediate Hypergraph Data Model",http://www.arc-mind.com/whitepapers/SpringIntroduction.pdf

[33] Wikipedia, "Control Flow", http://en.wikipedia.org/wiki/Control_flow

[34] I. Ankorion, "Change Data Capture – Efficient ETL for Real-Time BI",http://www.dmreview.com/editorial/dmreview/print_action.cfm?articleId=1016326

[35] Gregor Hohpe et al, "Enterprise Integration Patterns" Addison-Wesley, ISBN-10: 0321200683

[36] D. Bakken, "Middleware", http://www.eecs.wsu.edu/~bakken/middleware-article-bakken.pdf

[37] D. Winer "Bio",http://en.wikipedia.org/wiki/Dave_Winer

[38] Wikipedia "ebXML", http://en.wikipedia.org/wiki/EbXML

[39] D. Box, "A brief history of SOAP", http://webservices.xml.com/pub/a/ws/2001/04/04/soap.html

[40] M. Bernauer et al "Comparing WSDL-based and ebXML-based approaches for B2B protocol specifications". ICSOC 2003, http://www.big.tuwien.ac.at/research/publications/2003/1103-slides.pdf

[41] POJO: Plain Old Java Object

[42] BEA, IBM, Oracle, Microsoft (in alphabetical order)

[43] ICSOC, http://www.icsoc.org

[44] Alistair Barros et al "Service Interaction Patterns", http://sky.fit.qut.edu.au/~dumas/ServiceInteractionPatterns/patterns.html

[45] InnoQ, "Web Services Standards as of Q1 2007", http://www.innoq.com/soa/ws-standards/poster/

[46] M. Papazoglou et al "A Survey of Web service technologies", Technical Report, University of Trento, http://eprints.biblio.unitn.it/archive/00000586/

[47] M. Leroux Bustamente "Making Sense of all these Crazy Web Service Standards". InfoQ, http://www.infoq.com/articles/ws-standards-wcf-bustamante

[48] F. Leyman, "Jump Onto the Bus", Keynote, ICSOC 2003, http://www.unitn.it/convegni/download/icsoc03/keynote/P_Leymann.pdf

[49] R. Costello "Creating Variable Content Container Elements", http://www.xfront.org/variablecontentcontainer.pdf

[50] http://www.w3.org/TR/xmlschema-guide2versioning/#wildcard

[51] B. Lublinsky "Versioning in SOA", http://msdn2.microsoft.com/en-us/arcjournal/bb491124.aspx

[52] J.J. Dubray et al "An eXtensible Object Model for Business-to-Business eCommerce Systems", OOPSLA 1999, http://jeffsutherland.com/oopsla99/Dubray/dubray.html

[53] J.J. Dubray et al "An XML information server for advanced B2B architectures", http://www.gca.org/papers/xmleurope2000/pdf/s25-03.pdf

[54] Andrew Davidson "Schema For Object Oriented XML", W3C Note, http://www.w3.org/TR/NOTE-SOX/

[55] M. Yader et al "The Battle to Transport XML Business Documents",http://drrw.net/presentations/XML2002%20Baltimore/XML2002.ZIP

[56] Martin Fowler, "Inversion of Control Containers and the Dependency Injection Pattern", http://www.martinfowler.com/articles/injection.html

[57] Rod Johnson et al, Interface21, http://www.springframework.org/

[58] G. Hohpe, "Let's have a conversation", http://dsonline.computer.org/portal/site/dsonline/menuitem.9ed3d9924aeb0dcd82ccc6716bbe36ec/index.jsp?&pName=dso_level1&path=dsonline/2007/06&file=w3tow.xml&xsl=article.xsl&

[59] J.J. Dubray, "WS-Choreography Definition Language", http://www.ebpml.org/ws_-_cdl.htm

[60] G. Hohpe, "Conversation between loosely coupled systems". http://www.infoq.com/presentations/hohpe-soa-conversations

[61] B. Lublinsky, "Service Composition", http://www.infoq.com/articles/lublinsky-soa-composition

[62] WS-CAF, OASIS, http://www.oasis-open.org/committees/tc_home.php?wg_abbrev=ws-caf

[63] C. Barreto, "WS-BPEL v2.0 Primer", http://www.oasis-open.org/committees/download.php/23974/wsbpel-v2.0-primer.pdf

[64] OSGi Consortium, http://www.osgi.org

[65] J. McKendrick, "Do we need this animal called BPEL4People", http://www.webservices.org/weblog/joe_mckendrick/do_we_need_this_animal_called_bpel4people

[66] A. da Silva "Simplify WSDL Composition with the ETTK WSDL Port Type Aggregator", http://www.ibm.com/developerworks/webservices/library/ws-simplewsdl/

[67] S. Graham "Publish-Subscribe Notification for Web services", http://www.ibm.com/developerworks/library/ws-pubsub/WS-PubSub.pdf

[68] M. Humphrey, "An Early Evaluation of WSRF and WS-Notification via WSRF.NET", http://www.cs.virginia.edu/~gsw2c/WSRFdotNet/wsrf_Grid2004.pdf

[69] M. Weaver "Using WS-Notification", http://www.ibm.com/developerworks/grid/library/gr-ws-not/

[70] http://www.wsper.org

[71] A. Rotem-Gal-Oz "Bridging the gap between BI and SOA", http://www.infoq.com/articles/BI-and-SOA

[72] R. Schulte "The Growing Role of Events in Enterprise Applications", 2003 http://www.gartner.com/DisplayDocument?doc_cd=116129

[73] J.J. Dubray "WSPER: An Abract SOA Framework", http://www.wsper.org/primer.html

[74] V. Akhmechet "Erlang Style Concurrency", http://www.defmacro.org/ramblings/concurrency.html

[75] R. Kong "Transform WebSphere Business Modeler process Models to BPEL", www.ibm.com/developerworks/websphere/library/techarticles/0504_kong/0504_kong.html

[76] S. White et al "Business Process Modeling Notation Specification v1.0", http://www.bpmn.org/Documents/OMG%20Final%20Adopted%20BPMN%201-0%20Spec%202006-02-01.pdf

[77] "Enterprise Service Design Guide", SAP,
https://www.sdn.sap.com/irj/servlet/prt/portal/prtroot/docs/library/uuid/
943e83e5-0601-0010-acb5-b16258f5f20a

[78] ADP is a US corporation that provides employers with employee background checks

[79] G. Terrill "Are Mashups EAI 2.0", InfoQ.com 2007,
http://www.infoq.com/news/2007/08/mashups-eai-2

[80] M. Matsumura "SOA meets Web 2.0 at SOA executive forum",
InfoQ.com, http://www.infoq.com/news/SOA-Meets-Web-2.0-Panel-at-Infow

[81] J.J. Dubray "A Mashup to help young multilingual children learn how to read", http://www.flashreader.org/tour.aspx

[82] I am referring to the implementation level, not the logical level, the semantics of containment (aggregation, composition) are implemented at the DAL level, not within the ER implementation itself.

[83] R. Schulte, "The Growing Role of Events in Enterprise Applications",
http://www.gartner.com/DisplayDocument?doc_cd=116129

[84] J. Taylor, "Enterprise Decision Management Blog",
http://www.edmblog.com/weblog/

[85] R. Costello "Global vs Local",
http://www.xfront.com/GlobalVersusLocal.html

[86] S. Hu, "XML Schema considerations for WSDL design in conformation with WS-I Basic Profile ",
http://www.ibm.com/developerworks/webservices/library/ws-soa-xmlwsdl.html

[87] OASIS 9.0 Naming and Design Rules,
http://www.openapplications.org/downloads/oagis/loadfrm90NDR.htm

[88] D. Linthicum "Using a Common Data Model with SOA",
http://weblog.infoworld.com/realworldsoa/archives/2007/07/using_a_common.html

[89] D. Booth, "Web Services Architecture", http://www.w3.org/TR/ws-arch/#service_oriented_model

[90] J. van Hoof "How to mediate semantics in an EDA", http://soa-eda.blogspot.com/2007/04/how-to-mediate-semantics-in-eda.html

[91] D. Webber. "Bizcodes: Empowering the Internet",
http://www.touchbriefings.com/pdf/967/46.pdf

[92] SAP Developer Network, "UN/CEFACT Core Components Technical Specification",
https://www.sdn.sap.com/irj/sdn?rid=/webcontent/uuid/1baa57f9-0a01-0010-1684-c42a08982294

[93] G. Stuhec "How to Solve the Business Standards Dilemma – The CCTS Standards Stack",

https://www.sdn.sap.com/irj/sdn/go/portal/prtroot/docs/library/uuid/30d
35ece-5c67-2910-64aa-cb331726ee1c
[94] J.J. Moreau "What's new in WSDL 2.0",
http://www.idealliance.org/papers/dx_xmle04/slides/moreau.pdf
[95] R. Chinnici "WSDL v 2.0 Part 2: Adjuncts", W3C,
http://www.w3.org/TR/wsdl20-extensions/
[96] A. Lewis "WSDL v2.0: Additional MEPs",W3C,
http://www.w3.org/TR/2007/NOTE-wsdl20-additional-meps-
20070626/
[97] Choreology, "The Business Transaction Management Spectrum"
http://www.choreology.com/standards/standards_btm_spectrum.htm
[98] E. Newcomer et al "WS-AtomicTransaction", http://docs.oasis-
open.org/ws-tx/wstx-wsat-1.1-spec-os.pdf
[99] J.J. Dubray et al "OASIS ebBP Specification v2.0.4", http://docs.oasis-
open.org/ebxml-bp/2.0.4/ebxmlbp-v2.0.4-Spec-cs-en.pdf
[100] R. Butek "Which style of WSDL should I use?"
,http://www.ibm.com/developerworks/webservices/library/ws-
whichwsdl/
[101] Open Applications Group Development Methodology,
http://www.openapplications.org/downloads/developmentmethodology/
2006%20OAGi%20Development%20Methodology.pdf
[102] Wikipedia, "REpresentational State Transfer",
http://en.wikipedia.org/wiki/Representational_State_Transfer
[103] R. Costello, "Buiding a Web Service the REST way",
http://www.xfront.com/REST-Web-Services.html
[104] H. Wilms "Selling SOA to the business",
http://www.infoq.com/news/2007/08/selling-soa
[105] W. Keller "SOA Governance – Long term SOA Implementation and
Management", http://www.infoq.com/articles/keller-soa-governance
[106] J.J. Dubray, "Fundamentals of Service Orientation", Attachmate 2005,
http://www.attachmate.com/NR/rdonlyres/C44FE6A5-E23F-4FEC-
8A3B-5FA24A083A5D/0/050003_Fund_of_SO.pdf
[107] S. Tilkov "SOA Maturity Models",
http://www.infoq.com/news/2007/02/soa-maturity-models
[108] S. Inaganti, "SOA Maturity Model"
http://www.bptrends.com/publicationfiles/04-07-ART-
The%20SOA%20MaturityModel-Inagantifinal.pdf
[109] Lean Advisors Inc. "Lean Six Sigma Program ",
http://www.leanadvisors.com/lean_sixsigma_implementation.cfm
[110] Jon Bosak, ebXML mailing list, 2001

www.ingramcontent.com/pod-product-compliance
Lightning Source LLC
Chambersburg PA
CBHW051245050326
40689CB00007B/1078